THE MEDITERRANEAN SLOW COOKER COOKBOOK FOR BEGINNERS

250 QUICK AND EASY RECIPES FOR BUSY AND NOVICE THAT COOK THEMSELVES

2-WEEK MEAL PLAN INCLUDED

BY

WILDA BUCKLEY

TABLE OF CONTENTS

INTRODUCTION

The Mediterranean diet has been in practice in history for centuries.

Its origins can be traced to ancient Crete, Greece, Sicily, and southern Italy. It has always been associated with the healthy Mediterranean life style that produces long-lived people. Those who live a long fulfilling life are said to possess a little secret that gives them a longevity and serenity.

They do not suffer from such debilitating infirmities like heart problems, high blood pressure, Alzheimer's, stroke, and cancer. Their secret to longevity is the Mediterranean diet that they consume regularly.

For centuries the Mediterranean diet has kept people living a longer and healthier life style than others. The secret to long life is the diet's inclusion of ample vegetables, fruits, olive oil, and nuts. It is of the understanding that all vegetables and fruits, nuts, legumes, and fish are all rich in antioxidants that help the body combat the free radical damage that leads to inflammation and other diseases. Most importantly, they are rich in phytochemicals that help fight the various cancers in the body.

It is also observed that those who eat the Mediterranean way of life live a much healthier lifestyle. That's because of the simple fact that they do not suffer from obesity or obesity related conditions like diabetes 2 and heart diseases. They are active people and they burn off the excess calories so that they do not hoard them as fat in the body.

The Mediterranean diet is rich in foods that are good for the heart and blood vessels. They are also good for the proper function of the brain. This, therefore, aids in the brain's ability to affect the memory. This is why many people who have followed the Mediterranean way of life have lived for so long.

The diet can protect against a lot of infectious diseases, cancers, cardiovascular and neurodegenerative diseases. This being because of the high level of antioxidants in all the foods in the diet. A lack of these antioxidants in the body leads to a decreased immunity, reduced mental focus, and eventually Alzheimer's at some point in life.

Olive oil is the best source of monounsaturated fat that boost the HDL which stands for good cholesterol. Monounsaturated fat is also good as a heart lubricant. It helps protect the arteries from atherosclerosis. It also contains squalene, the anti-inflammatory and anti-cancer agent. Olive oil is also chocked full of antioxidants, crucial for a healthy body.

In addition, a common side effect of a monounsaturated fat is weight loss. That is because monounsaturated fat is better at filling the stomach than the saturated fat. The monounsaturated fat-filled stomach leads to a feeling of fullness, and this reduces the inclination to overeat. That is why people who follow the Mediterranean diet are not fat.

Among fruits, the grapefruit has a powerful compound called naringenin that was found effective in destroying one of the deadliest forms of cancer among women. Lemons are a rich source of phytochemicals that help prevent or reverse the damage caused by cancer and Alzheimer's. Strawberries are also packed with antioxidants and minerals that promote cardiovascular health.

Moreover, this diet is made for all, irrespective of age. Because of this, the diet is also beneficial for pregnant women because it helps to reduce the chances of having children that are born prematurely or underweight.
Nuts are also part of the diet as they help reduce heart disease, such as walnuts, also known to be effective in preventing colon cancer as well as some of the other cancers.

There are also fish, rich in omega-3 fatty acids. Among them is mackerel, salmon, and sardines. They are good for heart and brain health.

The diet also includes dairy and this was found to be helpful in combatting the risks of heart diseases as well as ailments like diabetes 2 and Alzheimer's.

Finally, the diet also includes wine and the right kind of alcohols. The wine traditions of the Mediterranean are many. Just like the diet itself, enjoying wine is one of the healthiest types of alcohols with a host of health benefits.

In modern times, people around the globe adopted the Mediterranean diet. In the US, the Mediterranean diet is viewed as a healthy, safe, and effective weight loss approach. It is promoted by the non-profit Oldways Preservation & Exchange Trust. The diet is based on the Mediterranean Diet Pyramid which was identified in the year 1992.

There were, however, critics of the diet. Some of them considered it to be too expensive to adhere to. Others felt that it was time-consuming when it came to cooking and preparation time.
But all and all, the Mediterranean diet is a great diet. It is tasty, delicious, and healthy at the same time.

1. Egg and Vegetable Breakfast Casserole

Preparation time: 15 minutes
Cooking time: 4 hours
Servings: 8

Ingredients:
- 8 eggs
- 4 egg whites
- ¾ cup milk (can use almond)
- 2 teaspoons stone-ground mustard
- ½ teaspoon garlic salt
- 1 teaspoon salt
- ½ teaspoon pepper
- 1 30-ounce bag frozen hash browns
- 4 strips cooked bacon (optional)
- ½ onion, roughly chopped
- 2 bell peppers, roughly chopped
- 1 small head of broccoli, roughly chopped
- 6 ounces cheddar cheese

Directions:
1. Mix the eggs, egg whites, milk, mustard, garlic salt, salt, and pepper until well combined.
2. Spray the inside of the slow cooker with olive oil.
3. Spread half of the hash browns bag across the slow cooker's bottom and then top with bacon.
4. Pour egg mixture over the bacon and potatoes. Add the onion, bell peppers, and broccoli, then top with remaining hash browns and cheese. Cook on low for 4 hours.

Nutrition: Calories 320 Fat 13 g Carbs 29 g Protein 22 g Sodium 700 mg

2. Breakfast Stuffed Peppers

Preparation time: 15 minutes
Cooking time: 4 hours
Servings: 4

Ingredients:
- ½ pound ground breakfast sausage
- 4 bell peppers
- 6 large eggs
- 4 ounces Monterey Jack Cheese, shredded
- 4 ounces fire-roasted chopped green chilies
- ¼ teaspoon salt
- 1/8 teaspoon pepper

Directions:
1. Slice the peppers off the tops and clean out the seeds.
2. Brown the sausage in a skillet. Beat your eggs until fluffy in a mixing bowl. Then mix in the cheese and green chilies.
3. Put salt plus pepper in the egg mixture. Spray the slow cooker with olive oil and place the peppers inside.
4. Put the egg mixture on each pepper to the top. Set your slow cooker to high within 2 hours, or cook on low for 4 hours. Serve when the egg mixture is set.

Nutrition: Calories 261 Fat 16.8 g Carbs 9.2 g Protein 17.3 g Sodium 401 mg

3. Slow Cooker Frittata

Preparation time: 15 minutes
Cooking time: 2 hours
Servings: 6

Ingredients:
- 1 (14-ounce) can small artichoke hearts, drained and cut into bite-sized pieces
- 1 jar roasted red peppers, bite-sized pieces
- ¼ cup sliced green onions
- 8 eggs, beaten
- 4 ounces crumbled Feta cheese
- 1 teaspoon seasoning salt
- ½ teaspoon pepper
- ¼ cup chopped cilantro

Directions:
1. Spray the slow cooker with olive oil and add the artichoke hearts, red peppers, and green onions.
2. Put the beaten eggs over the top of the vegetables and stir to combine. Season the mixture with pepper and seasoning salt.
3. Mix in the chopped cilantro. Top with Feta cheese. Cook on low within 2–3 hours or until set.

Nutrition: Calories 243 Fat 14.5 g Carbs 12.7g Protein 15.4 g Sodium 364 mg

4. Cranberry Apple Oatmeal

Preparation time: 15 minutes
Cooking time: 6 hours
Servings: 4

Ingredients:
- 4 cups of water
- 2 cups old-fashioned oats
- ½ cup dried cranberries
- 2 apples, peeled and diced
- ¼ cup brown sugar
- 2 tablespoons butter, melted
- ½ teaspoon salt
- 1 teaspoon cinnamon

Directions:
1. Grease your slow cooker using a nonstick cooking spray. Put all of the fixings in the slow cooker and stir to combine.
2. Cook on low for 3 hours. If you want to prepare this the night before, you can cook it for up to 6 hours. Serve.

Nutrition: Calories 254 Fat 7.2 g Carbs 40.9 g Protein 6.4 g Sodium 138 mg

5. Blueberry Banana Steel Cut Oats

Preparation time: 15 minutes
Cooking time: 8 hours
Servings: 4

Ingredients:
- 1 cup steel-cut oats
- 2 ripe bananas, sliced or mashed
- 1–2 cups fresh or frozen blueberries
- 2 cups of water
- 2 cups milk (almond milk works very well in this recipe)
- 2 tablespoons honey or pure maple syrup
- ¼ teaspoon salt
- 1 teaspoon cinnamon
- 2 teaspoons vanilla
- Optional add-ins: chopped nuts, nut butter, fresh or dried fruit, granola, shredded coconut, honey, additional milk

Directions:
1. Grease your slow cooker using a nonstick cooking spray. Add all the fixings to the slow cooker and mix well. Cook on low overnight for 6–8 hours or cook on high for 2–3 hours.

Nutrition: Calories 297 Fat 4.4 g Carbs 58 g Protein 8 g Sodium 81 mg

6. Berry Breakfast Quinoa

Preparation time: 15 minutes
Cooking time: 3 hours
Servings: 5

Ingredients:
- 1 large avocado, pitted and mashed (you can replace with bananas)
- 4 cups of water
- 2 cups quinoa, rinsed
- 2 cups fresh mixed berries
- 2 tablespoons pure maple syrup
- 2 teaspoons vanilla
- 1 teaspoon cinnamon
- ¼ teaspoon salt

Directions:
1. Spray your slow cooker using a nonstick cooking spray. Put all the listed ingredients in the slow cooker and mix well.
2. Cook on low for 5 hours or high for 2–3 hours. Serve.

Nutrition: Calories 229 Fat 2.8 g Carbs 44 g Protein 7 g Sodium 90 mg

Mediterranean Crockpot Breakfast

Preparation Time: 15 minutes
Cooking Time: 7 hours
Servings: 8

Ingredients:
- Eggs - 1 dozen
- Hash brown potatoes - 2 pounds
- Milk - 1 cup
- Shredded cheddar cheese - 3 cups
- Diced onions - ½ cup
- Bacon – 1 pound
- Garlic powder - ¼ teaspoon
- Dry mustard - ¼ teaspoon
- Salt - 1 teaspoon
- Pepper - ½ teaspoon
- Spring onions – for garnishing

Directions:
1. Beat the eggs using a blender until they get combined well with one another
2. Now add garlic powder, milk, salt, mustard, and pepper along with the beaten eggs and continue blending. Keep aside.
3. Season the hash brown potatoes with pepper and salt. Place the hash brown potatoes in a layer by layer and diced onions into the crockpot.
4. Sprinkle a quarter portion of bacon and mix them well. Add a cup of cheese to the crockpot to make it a smooth looking texture.

5. Repeat this layering process two to three times. Now pour the blended egg mixture over the layers of hash potatoes in the crockpot.
6. Set slow cooking for 7 hours. Garnish with finely chopped spring onions while serving.

Nutrition: Calories: 245 Carbs: 16g Fat: 8g Protein: 24g

7. Slow Cooker Mediterranean Potatoes

Preparation Time: 5 minutes
Cooking Time: 5 hours
Servings: 8
Ingredients:

- Fingerling potatoes - 3 pounds
- Dried oregano - 1 tablespoon
- Olive oil - 2 tablespoons
- Smoked paprika - 1 teaspoon
- Unsalted butter - 2 tablespoons
- Ground black pepper, fresh – 1 teaspoon
- Lemon juice - 1 teaspoon
- Minced garlic - 4 cloves
- Fresh parsley leaves, chopped - 2 tablespoons
- Kosher salt - ½ teaspoon
- Lemon - 1 zest

Directions:

1. Peel, wash potatoes, and cut into half. Keep aside. Slightly grease the inside of a 6-quart slow cooker with nonstick spray.
2. Add olive oil, potatoes, lemon juice, butter, paprika, and oregano in the cooker. Season by using pepper and salt
3. Close the lid. Set it to slow cook within 5 hours. Serve hot by garnishing with chopped parsley and lemon zest.

Nutrition: Calories: 149 Carbs: 23g Fat: 5g Protein: 3g

8. Mediterranean Crockpot Quiche

Preparation Time: 15 minutes
Cooking Time: 6 hours
Servings: 9

Ingredients:

- Milk – 1 cup
- Eggs – 8
- Feta cheese, crumbled - 1½ cup
- Bisquick mix – 1 cup
- Spinach, fresh, chopped – 2 cups
- Red bell pepper - ½ cup
- Garlic, nicely chopped – 1 teaspoon
- Basil leaves, fresh - ¼ cup
- Sausage crumbles fully cooked – 9.6 ounces

- Feta cheese, crumbled (for garnishing) - ¼ cup

Directions:

1. Grease a 5-quart slow cooker using a cooking spray. In a large bowl, whisk eggs, Bisquick mix and milk thoroughly.
2. Add one and half crumbled feta cheese, garlic, basil, sausage, bell pepper, and thoroughly stir the entire mix.
3. Close the lid and set slow cooking for 6 hours. Cut into pieces for serving. Garnish with feta cheese sprinkling.

Nutrition: Calories: 321 Carbs: 26g Fat: 22g Protein: 2g

9. Slow Cooker Meatloaf

Preparation Time: 15 minutes
Cooking Time: 4 hours
Servings: 4

Ingredients:

- Minced beef - ½ pound
- Tomato sauce – 2 cups
- Onion, diced - 1 small
- Bacon unsmoked - 4
- Red wine - ½ cup
- Mustard - 1 teaspoon
- Cheddar cheese - 1 oz.
- Oregano - 1 teaspoon
- Garlic puree - 1 teaspoon
- Thyme - 1 teaspoon
- Paprika - 1 teaspoon
- Salt - ½ teaspoon
- Pepper - ½ teaspoon
- Parsley - 1 teaspoon
- Fresh herbs – as required

Directions:

1. In a large bowl, put all the seasoning items. Add onion and minced beef to the bowl and mix well by combing with your hands.
2. Spread the mixture on a clean worktop and press it forms like a pastry, which can roll out cleanly.
3. In the middle portion of the meatloaf pastry, layer some chopped cheese. After adding the cheese as a layer, wrap the meat like a sausage roll.
4. Pour little olive oil into the slow cooker for greasing and then place the roll. Mix homemade tomato sauce and red wine in a separate bowl and pour it on the meatloaf's sides.
5. Do not pour this mixture over the meatloaf. Now, spread the bacon over the meatloaf. Slow cook it for four hours. Serve hot along with roast vegetables and potatoes.

Nutrition: Calories: 234 Carbs: 17g Fat: 6g Protein: 27g

10. Crock Pot Chicken Noodle Soup

Preparation Time: 15 minutes
Cooking Time: 6 hours
Servings: 4

Ingredients:

- Chicken breasts, boneless and skinless, cut into ½" size – 3
- Chicken broth - 5½ cup
- Chopped celery stalks - 3
- Chopped carrots - 3
- Chopped onion - 1
- Bay leaf - 1
- Minced garlic cloves - 3
- Peas, frozen - 1 cup
- Egg noodles - 2½ cup
- Fresh parsley, chopped - ¼ cup
- Ground black pepper, fresh - ½ teaspoon
- Salt - ½ teaspoon

Directions:

1. Put and arrange the chicken breasts in the bottom of the slow cooker. On top of the chicken, put onion, celery stalks, garlic cloves, and carrots.
2. Pour in the chicken broth and put the bay leaf in. Add pepper and salt as per your taste.
3. Cook on slow cook mode for 6 hours. After six hours, add egg noodles and frozen peas to the cooker.
4. Cook further about 5-6 minutes until the egg noodles turn tender. Stir in chopped fresh parsley. Serve hot.

Nutrition: Calories: 150 Carbs: 10g Fat: 6g Protein: 13g

11. Hash Brown & Cheddar Breakfast

Preparation Time: 30 minutes
Cooking Time: 6 hours
Servings: 12

Ingredients:

- Hash browns, frozen & shredded - 32 ounces
- Onion, green, coarsely chopped - 6
- Breakfast sausage, crumbled & cooked - 16 ounces
- Eggs - 12
- Shredded cheddar cheese - 12 ounces
- Garlic powder - ¼ teaspoon
- Milk - ¼ cup
- Pepper - ½ teaspoon
- Salt - 1 teaspoon
- Pepper – 1 teaspoon for seasoning.
- Salt - ½ teaspoon for seasoning.

Directions:

1. Oil a 6-quart slow cooker with nonstick cooking spray. In the slow cooker, layer 1/3 portion of hash brown.
2. Season this layer with pepper and salt. Now, layer 1/3 portion of the cooked and crumbled sausage over the first layer.
3. Again layer 1/3 portion of both cheddar cheese and green onions over the sausage. Repeat both these layers twice, ending with cheese
4. Take a large bowl and whisk milk, egg, salt, garlic powder, and pepper. Pour this egg mixture all over the sausage, hash brown and cheese layers in the slow cooker.
5. Slow cook it for about six to eight hours until the edges turn brown, and the center becomes firm. Serve hot.

Nutrition: Calories: 150 Carbs: 17g Fat: 9g Protein: 1g

12. Slow Cooker Fava Beans

Preparation Time: 10 minutes
Cooking Time: 8 hours
Servings: 12

Ingredients:

- Fava beans (dried) - 1 pound
- Red lentils – 3 tablespoons
- Uncooked rice – 3 tablespoons
- Tomato, chopped - 1
- Garlic, chopped – 3 cloves
- Water – as required (about 2 cups)
- Salt - ½ teaspoon
- For sausage:
- Onion, finely sliced in rings - ½
- Tomato – 1 small
- Olive oil – 2 tablespoons
- Sausages, cut into halves – 4
- Cumin seed - ¼ teaspoon
- Lemon juice - ½ teaspoon

Directions:

1. Soak the fava beans for about 4 hours. Wash and drain the beans. Put the drained beans in a 6-quart slow cooker.
2. Wash the lentils, rice, and drain. Put the drained lentils and rice also into the slow cooker. Now add the chopped tomato and garlic into the slow cooker.
3. Add water above the ingredients level. Set the slow cooking for 8 hours. When cooking over, prepare the sausages. Pour olive oil into a nonstick pan and bring to heat at a medium-high temperature.
4. When the oil becomes hot, add chopped onions and sauté on medium heat until it becomes tender.

Now add chopped garlic and continue stirring until the fragrance starts to release. Add cumin seeds and continue stirring.

5. After that, add chopped tomatoes and sausages. Continue stirring for 5 minutes. Now transfer the cooked beans over the sausages.
6. Drizzle the lemon juice over the beans. Add salt if required. Stir the mix and cook for 2-3 minutes to warm the food. Serve hot.

Nutrition: Calories: 88 Carbs: 18g Fat: 1g Protein: 8g

13. Pork Sausage Breakfast

Preparation Time: 15 minutes
Cooking Time: 6 hours
Servings: 12

Ingredients:

- Pork sausage - 16 ounce
- Eggs - 12
- Milk - 1 cup
- Veg oil – 2 tablespoons
- Hash brown potatoes, frozen - 26 ounces
- Ground mustard - 1 tablespoon
- Ground black pepper - as per the taste required
- Cheddar cheese, shredded - 16 ounces.
- Salt - ½ teaspoon
- Pepper - ¾ teaspoon
- Cooking spray – as required

Directions:

1. Spray some nonstick cooking oil into the bottom of your crockpot. Layer the hash brown potatoes in the crockpot.
2. Now pour vegetable oil into a large skillet and heat on medium-high temperature. When the oil becomes hot, put the sausages in, stir and continue cooking for 7 minutes until it becomes brown and crumbly.
3. Once the cooking is over, remove the sausage and discard the oil. Now, spread the sausage over the hash brown potatoes and top it with cheddar cheese.
4. Beat milk and eggs in a separate large bowl. Add ground mustard along with salt and pepper to this mixture and stir thoroughly. Pour this batter on top of the cheese layer. Set on a slow cook for six hours. Serve hot.

Nutrition: Calories: 290 Carbs: 1g Fat: 24g Protein: 10g

14. Butcher Style Cabbage Rolls – Pork & Beef Version

Preparation time: 15 minutes
Cooking time: 8.5 hours
Servings: 6

Ingredients:
- 1 large head of white cabbage – 3 pounds
- 1 ¾ cups beef, chopped into small pieces
- 1 ¾ cups pork, chopped into small pieces
- 1 sweet onion, cut into small pieces
- 1 red bell pepper, cubes
- 1 cup mushrooms, chopped small
- 2 Tablespoons olive oil
- 1 cup beef broth
- ½ cup cooking cream
- Salt and pepper to taste
- 1 heaping teaspoon ground cumin

Directions:
1. Cut out the stalk of the cabbage head like a cone shape, place the cabbage in a pot with the hole up, boil some water and pour it over the cabbage. Let it soak in hot water within 10 minutes. Chop the meats into small pieces; place them in a mixing bowl.
2. In a pan, heat the olive oil. Sauté the onion, the bell pepper, and the mushrooms for 5 minutes, cool them in the pan, and add to the meats.
3. Add the seasoning, mix well with your hands. Separate 8-10 leaves of cabbage, lay each one flat, cut the thick part of the stalk, and stuff the leaf with about 2 tablespoons of meat mixture.
4. Roll and put aside until the meat mixture is used up. Finely cut the remaining cabbage and place it in the crockpot. Place the prepared cabbage rolls seam-side down, pour the broth and the cream evenly over the cabbage rolls. Cover, cook on low within 8.5 hours.

Nutrition: Calories: 130 Carbs: 10g Fat: 6g Protein: 9g

15. One-Pot Oriental Lamb

Preparation time: 15 minutes
Cooking time: 4 hours
Servings: 4

Ingredients:
- 3 cups lamb, de-boned and diced
- 2 Tablespoons almond flower
- 2 cups fresh spinach
- 4 small red onions, halved
- 2 garlic cloves, minced
- ¼ cup yellow turnip, diced
- 2 Tablespoons dry sherry
- 2-3 bay leaves
- 1 teaspoon hot mustard
- ¼ teaspoon ground nutmeg
- 1 teaspoon chopped fresh thyme
- 1 teaspoon chopped fresh rosemary
- 5-6 whole pimento berries
- 1 1/3 cups broth of your choice – beef, chicken, or lamb
- Salt and pepper to taste
- 8 baby zucchinis, halved
- 2 Tablespoons olive oil

Directions:
1. Preheat the crockpot on high. Place the lamb in the crockpot, cover with almond flour. Add the remaining ingredients to the crockpot. Cover, cook on high for 4 hours. Serve.

Nutrition: Calories: 356 Carbs: 9g Fat: 24g Protein: 27g

16. Zucchini Lasagna with Minced Pork

Preparation time: 15 minutes
Cooking time: 8 hours
Servings: 6

Ingredients:
- 4 medium-sized zucchinis
- 1 small onion, diced
- 1 garlic clove, minced
- 2 cups lean ground pork, minced
- 2 regular cans diced Italian tomatoes
- 2 Tablespoons olive oil
- 2 cups grated Mozzarella cheese
- 1 egg
- Small bunch of fresh basil or 1 Tablespoon dry basil
- Salt and pepper to taste
- 2 Tablespoons butter to grease crockpot

Directions:
1. Cut the zucchini lengthwise, making 6 slices from each vegetable. Salt and let drain. Discard the liquid.
2. In a pan, heat the olive oil. Sauté the onion and garlic within 5 minutes. Add minced meat and cook for another 5 minutes. Put tomatoes and simmer within 5 minutes.
3. Add seasoning and mix well. Add basil leaves. Cool slightly. Beat the egg, mix in 1 cup of cheese.

4. Grease the crockpot with butter and start layering the lasagna. First, the zucchini slices, then a layer of meat mixture, top it with cheese, and repeat. Finish with zucchini and the second cup of cheese. Cover, cook on low for 8 hours.

Nutrition: Calories: 168 Carbs: 5g Fat: 11g Protein: 16g

17. <u>Stuffed Bell Peppers Dolma Style</u>

Preparation time: 15 minutes
Cooking time: 6 hours
Servings: 6

Ingredients:

- 1 cup lean ground beef
- 1 ¾ cup lean ground pork
- 1 small white onion, diced
- 6 bell peppers in various colors
- 1 small head cauliflower
- 1 small can tomato paste – 28 ounces
- 4 garlic cloves, crushed
- 2 Tablespoons olive oil
- Salt and pepper to taste
- 1 Tablespoon dried thyme

Directions:

1. Cut off tops of the bell peppers, set aside. Clean inside the peppers. Chop the cauliflower into tiny pieces resembling rice grains, place in a mixing bowl.
2. Add the onion, crushed garlic, dried herbs. Combine thoroughly. Add the meats, tomato paste, and seasoning. Mix well with your hands.
3. Sprinkle olive oil along the bottom and sides of the crockpot. Stuff the bell peppers with the mixture and set them in the crockpot. Carefully place the top back on each pepper. Cover, cook on low for 6 hours.

Nutrition: Calories: 200 Carbs: 26g Fat: 6g Protein: 10g

18. <u>Slow BBQ Ribs</u>

Preparation time: 15 minutes
Cooking time: 8 hours
Servings: 6

Ingredients:

- 3 pounds pork ribs
- 1 Tablespoon of olive oil
- 1 small can ounces tomato paste – 28 ounces
- ½ cup hot water
- ½ cup vinegar
- 6 Tablespoons Worcestershire sauce
- 4 Tablespoons dry mustard
- 1 Tablespoon chili powder

- 1 heaping teaspoon ground cumin
- 1 teaspoon powdered Swerve (or a suitable substitute)
- Salt and pepper to taste

Directions:

1. Warm-up, the olive oil in a frying pan, then brown the ribs on both sides. Add them to the crockpot.
2. Combine the rest of the fixing in a bowl, blend well. Pour over the ribs - coat all sides. Cover, cook on low for 8 hours.

Nutrition: Calories: 243 Carbs: 8g Fat: 15g Protein: 19g

19. <u>Steak and Salsa</u>

Preparation time: 15 minutes
Cooking time: 8 hours
Servings: 6

Ingredients:

- 2 ½ cups salsa made of:
- 2 big beef tomatoes, diced
- 1 tablespoon olive oil
- 1 small red onion finely diced
- ½ bunch of cilantros, chopped
- Salt and pepper to taste
- 2 pounds stewing beef, sliced in strips
- 2 bell peppers, cut into strips
- 1 onion, sliced in semi-circles
- 4 tablespoons butter
- 2 tablespoons of mixed dry seasoning:
- 1 teaspoon ground cumin
- ½ teaspoon sweet paprika
- ½ teaspoon paprika flakes
- 1 teaspoon garlic salt
- ½ teaspoon fresh ground black pepper

Directions:

1. Cover the bottom of the crockpot with the salsa. Add remaining ingredients and mix well. Cover, cook on low for 6-8 hours. Serve.

Nutrition: Calories: 480 Carbs: 1g Fat: 39g Protein: 31g

21. Beef Pot Roast with Turnips

Preparation time: 15 minutes
Cooking time: 7 hours
Servings: 6

Ingredients:

- 3 pounds beef, chuck shoulder roast
- 2 Tablespoons olive oil
- 1 red onion, cut into small pieces
- 1 cup beef broth + 2 cups hot water
- 4 Tablespoons butter
- 1 teaspoon dry rosemary
- 1 teaspoon dry thyme
- Salt and pepper to taste
- 5 medium turnips, peeled, cut into strips

Directions:

1. Warm-up, the olive oil in your frying pan, then brown your meat for 2 minutes on each side. Pour the broth and remaining ingredients, without the turnips, into the crockpot.
2. Cover, cook on low for 5 hours. Take the lid off and quickly add the turnip strips. Re-cover, cook for an additional 2 hours on low, until the turnips are soft.

Nutrition: Calories: 462 Carbs: 10g Fat: 27g Protein: 6g

22. Chili Beef Stew

Preparation time: 15 minutes
Cooking time: 8 hours
Servings: 6

Ingredients:

- 3 pounds stewing beef, whole
- 2 cans Italian diced tomatoes
- 1 cup beef broth
- 4 Tablespoons butter
- 1 teaspoon Cayenne pepper
- 1 Tablespoon Worcestershire sauce
- 1 teaspoon dry oregano
- 1 teaspoon dry thyme
- Salt and pepper to taste

Directions:

1. Add all the fixing to the crockpot, mix well. Cover, cook on high for 6 hours.
2. Break up the beef with a fork, pull apart in the crockpot. Taste and adjust the seasoning, if needed. Re-cover, cook for an additional 2 hours on low.

Nutrition: Calories: 385 Carbs: 52g Fat: 6g Protein: 29g

23. Pork Shoulder Roast

Preparation time: 15 minutes
Cooking time: 8 hours
Servings: 6

Ingredients:

- 3 pounds pork shoulder, whole
- 1 can Italian diced tomatoes
- 1 sweet onion, diced
- 3 garlic cloves, diced
- 4 Tablespoons lard
- 1 cup of water
- 1 bay leaf
- ¼ teaspoon ground cloves
- Salt and pepper to taste

Directions:

1. Place meat in crockpot, pour water, and tomatoes over it, so the liquid covers 1/3 of the meat. Add remaining ingredients. Cover, cook on low for 8 hours. Serve.

Nutrition: Calories: 240 Carbs: 0g Fat: 17g Protein: 18g

24. Easy and Delicious Chicken Stew

Preparation time: 15 minutes
Cooking time: 5 hours
Servings: 6

Ingredients:

- pounds chicken thighs, de-boned and cubed
- 1 cup chicken broth + 1 cup hot water
- 3 diced celery sticks (approximately 1 ½ cups)
- 2 cups fresh spinach
- 1 red onion, diced
- 2 garlic cloves, minced
- 1 teaspoon dry oregano
- 1 teaspoon dry thyme
- 1 teaspoon dried rosemary
- 1 cup cooking cream
- Salt and pepper to taste

Directions:

1. Add all the ingredients to the crockpot. Cover, cook on low for 5 hours. Serve.

Nutrition: Calories: 232 Carbs: 17g Fat: 9g Protein: 22g

26. Chili Con Steak

Preparation time: 15 minutes
Cooking time: 6 hours
Servings: 6

Ingredients:
- 3 pounds beef steak, cubed
- 1 Tablespoon paprika
- ½ teaspoon chili powder
- 1 teaspoon dried oregano
- ½ teaspoon ground cumin
- Salt and pepper to taste
- 4 Tablespoons butter
- ½ cup sliced leeks
- 2 cups Italian diced tomatoes
- 1 cup broth, beef

Directions:
1. Place all the ingredients in the crockpot by order on the list. Stir. Cover, cook on high for 6 hours. Serve.

Nutrition: Calories: 290 Carbs: 5g Fat: 6g Protein: 28g

27. One-Pot Chicken and Green Beans

Preparation time: 15 minutes
Cooking time: 8 hours
Servings: 6

Ingredients:
- 2 cups green beans, trimmed
- 2 large beef tomatoes, diced
- 1 red onion, diced
- 2 garlic cloves, minced
- 1 bunch chopped fresh dill (around 1/8 cup)
- 1 lemon, juiced
- 4 Tablespoons butter
- 1 cup chicken broth
- 6 chicken thighs, skin on
- Salt and pepper to taste
- 2 Tablespoons olive oil

Directions:
1. Add all the listed ingredients to the slow cooker in order on the list. Brush chicken thighs with olive oil; season with salt and pepper.
2. Cover, cook on low for 8 hours. When ready, if desired, take the chicken out and crisp it under a broiler for a few minutes.

Nutrition: Calories: 317 Carbs: 27g Fat: 2g Protein: 30g

28. Two-Meat Chili

Preparation time: 15 minutes
Cooking time: 6 hours & 30 minutes
Servings: 6

Ingredients:
- 1 ½ cups lean ground pork sausage meat
- 1 ¾ cups stewing beef, cubed
- 2 Tablespoons olive oil
- 1 bell pepper, sliced
- 1 white onion, cut in semi-circles
- 1 cup beef broth
- 2 Tablespoons tomato paste
- 2 Tablespoons sweet paprika
- 1 teaspoon chili powder
- 1 teaspoon cumin
- 1 teaspoon oregano
- Salt and pepper to taste

Directions:
1. In a pan, heat the olive oil. Brown, the beef, transfer to the crockpot. Then, brown the sausage and transfer to crockpot.
2. In the same pan, sweat the onion and pepper slices for 4-5 minutes, pour over the meat. Add remaining ingredients to crockpot. Cover, cook on low for 6 hours. Turn to high, remove the lid and let the liquid reduce for 30 minutes.

Nutrition: Calories: 240 Carbs: 0g Fat: 17g Protein: 21g

29. Slightly Addictive Pork Curry

Preparation time: 15 minutes
Cooking time: 8 hours
Servings: 6

Ingredients:
- pounds pork shoulder, cubed
- 1 Tablespoon coconut oil
- 1 yellow onion, diced
- 2 garlic cloves, minced
- 2 Tablespoons tomato paste
- 1 small can coconut milk – 12 ounces
- 1 cup of water
- ½ cup white wine
- 1 teaspoon turmeric
- 1 teaspoon ginger powder
- 1 teaspoon curry powder
- ½ teaspoon paprika
- Salt and pepper to taste

Directions:
1. In a pan, heat 1 tablespoon olive oil. Sauté the onion and garlic for 2-3 minutes. Add the pork and brown it. Finish with tomato paste.
2. In the crockpot, mix all remaining ingredients, submerge the meat in the liquid. Cover, cook on low for 8 hours.

Nutrition: Calories: 110 Carbs: 11g Fat: 6g Protein: 2g

30. Greek Style Lamb Shanks

Preparation time: 15 minutes
Cooking time: 6 hours
Servings: 8

Ingredients:
- 3 Tablespoons butter
- 4 lamb shanks, approximately 1 pound each
- 2 Tablespoons olive oil
- 8-10 pearl onions
- 5 garlic cloves, minced
- 2 beef tomatoes, cubed
- ¼ cup of green olives
- 4 bay leaves
- 1 sprig fresh rosemary
- 1 teaspoon dry thyme
- 1 teaspoon ground cumin
- 1 cup fresh spinach
- ¾ cup hot water
- ½ cup red wine, Merlot or Cabernet
- Salt and pepper to taste

Directions:
1. In a pan, melt the butter, brown the shanks on each side. Remove from pan, add oil, onions, garlic. Cook for 3-4 minutes. Add tomatoes, olives, spices. Stir well.
2. Add liquids and return the meat. Bring to boil for 1 minute. Transfer everything to the crockpot. Cover, cook on medium-high for 6 hours.

Nutrition: Calories: 250 Carbs: 3g Fat: 16g Protein: 22g

31. Homemade Meatballs and Spaghetti Squash

Preparation time: 15 minutes
Cooking time: 8 hours
Servings: 8

Ingredients:
- 1 medium-sized spaghetti squash, washed
- 1 Tablespoon butter to grease crockpot
  - pounds lean ground beef
- 2 garlic cloves
- 1 red onion, chopped
- ½ cup almond flour
- 2 Tablespoons of dry Parmesan cheese
- 1 egg, beaten
- 1 teaspoon ground cumin
- Salt and pepper to taste
- 4 cans diced Italian tomatoes
- 1 small can tomato paste, 28 ounces
- 1 cup hot water
- 1 red onion, chopped
- ¼ cup chopped parsley
- ½ teaspoon each, salt and sugar (optional)
- 1 bay leaf

Directions:
1. Scoop out the seeds of the spaghetti squash with a spoon. Grease the crockpot, place both halves open side down in the crockpot. Mix meatball ingredients in a bowl. Form approximately 20 small meatballs.
2. In a pan, heat the olive oil. Brown the meatballs within 2-3 minutes on each side. Transfer to the crockpot.
3. In the small bowl, add the tomatoes, tomato paste, oil, water, onion, and parsley, add ½ teaspoon each of salt and sugar. Mix well. Pour the marinara sauce in the crockpot around the squash halves. Cover, cook on low for 8 hours.

Nutrition: Calories: 409 Carbs: 31g Fat: 18g Protein: 32g

32. Beef and Cabbage Roast

Preparation time: 15 minutes
Cooking time: 8 hours
Servings: 10

Ingredients:
- 1 red onion, quartered
- 2 garlic cloves, minced
- 2-3 stocks celery, diced (approximately 1 cup)
- 4-6 dry pimento berries
- 2 bay leaves
  - pounds beef brisket (two pieces)
- 1 teaspoon chili powder
- 1 teaspoon ground cumin
- 2 cups broth, beef + 2 cups hot water
- Salt and pepper to taste
- 1 medium cabbage (approximately 2.2 pounds), cut in half, then quartered

Directions:
1. Add all ingredients, except cabbage, to the crockpot in order of the list. Cover, cook on low for 7 hours. Uncover, add the cabbage on top of the stew. Re-cover, cook for 1 additional hour.

Nutrition: Calories: 283 Carbs: 15g Fat: 11g Protein: 26g

33. Simple Chicken Chili

Preparation time: 15 minutes
Cooking time: 6 hours
Servings: 8

Ingredients:

- 1 Tablespoon butter
- 1 red onion, sliced
- 1 bell pepper, sliced
- 2 garlic cloves, minced
- 3 pounds boneless chicken thighs
- 8 slices bacon, chopped
- 1 teaspoon chili powder
- Salt and pepper to taste
- 1 cup chicken broth
- ¼ cup of coconut milk
- 3 Tablespoons tomato paste

Directions:

1. Add all ingredients to the crockpot, starting with the butter. Cover, cook on low for 6 hours. Shred cooked the chicken using a fork in the crockpot. Serve.

Nutrition: Calories: 230 Carbs: 17g Fat: 6g Protein: 27g

34. Beef Shoulder in BBQ Sauce

Preparation time: 15 minutes
Cooking time: 10 hours
Servings: 12

Ingredients:

- 8 pounds beef shoulder, whole
- 1 Tablespoon butter
- 1 yellow onion, diced
- 1 garlic bulb, peeled and minced
- 4 Tablespoons red wine vinegar
- 2 Tablespoons Worcestershire sauce
- 4 Tablespoons Swerve (or a suitable substitute)
- 1 Tablespoon mustard
- 1 teaspoon salt
- 1 teaspoon fresh ground black pepper

Directions:

1. In a bowl, mix seasoning, then reserve aside. Dissolve the butter in your pan, add the meat. Brown on all sides. Transfer to crockpot. Fry the onion for 2-3 minutes in the same pan pours over the meat. Pour in the seasoning.
2. Cover, cook on low for 10 hours. Remove, then place on a platter, cover with foil, let it rest for 1 hour. Turn the crockpot on high, reduce the remaining liquid by half and serve with the shredded beef.

Nutrition: Calories: 140 Carbs: 5g Fat: 9g Protein: 8g

35. Moist and Spicy Pulled Chicken Breast

Preparation time: 15 minutes
Cooking time: 6 hours
Servings: 8

Ingredients:

- 1 teaspoon dry oregano
- 1 teaspoon dry thyme
- 1 teaspoon dried rosemary
- 1 teaspoon garlic powder
- 1 teaspoon sweet paprika
- ½ teaspoon chili powder
- Salt and pepper to taste
- 4 tablespoons butter
  - pounds of chicken breasts
- 1 ½ cups ready-made tomato salsa
- 2 Tablespoons of olive oil

Directions:

1. Mix dry seasoning, sprinkle half on the bottom of crockpot. Place the chicken breasts over it, spread the rest of the spices. Pour the salsa over the chicken. Cover, cook on low for 6 hours.

Nutrition: Calories: 184 Carbs: 0g Fat: 0g Protein: 22g

36. Whole Roasted Chicken

Preparation time: 15 minutes
Cooking time: 8 hours
Servings: 6

Ingredients:

- 1 whole chicken (approximately 5.5 pounds)
- 4 garlic cloves
- 6 small onions
- 1 Tablespoon olive oil, for rubbing
- 2 teaspoons salt
- 2 teaspoons sweet paprika
- 1 teaspoon Cayenne pepper
- 1 teaspoon onion powder
- 1 teaspoon ground thyme
- 2 teaspoons fresh ground black pepper
- 4 Tablespoons butter, cut into cubes

Directions:

1. Mix all dry ingredients well. Stuff the chicken belly with garlic and onions. On the bottom of the crockpot, place four balls of aluminum foil.
2. Set the chicken on top of the balls. Rub it generously with olive oil. Cover the chicken with seasoning, drop in butter pieces. Cover, cook on low for 8 hours.

Nutrition: Calories: 240 Carbs: 0g Fat: 17g Protein: 21g

37. Pot Roast Beef Brisket

Preparation time: 15 minutes
Cooking time: 12 hours
Servings: 10

Ingredients:
- o   pounds beef brisket, whole
- 2 Tablespoons olive oil
- 2 Tablespoons apple cider vinegar
- 1 teaspoon dry oregano
- 1 teaspoon dry thyme
- 1 teaspoon dried rosemary
- 2 Tablespoons paprika
- 1 teaspoon Cayenne pepper
- 1 tablespoon salt
- 1 teaspoon fresh ground black pepper

Directions:
1. In a bowl, mix dry seasoning, add olive oil, apple cider vinegar. Place the meat in the crockpot, generously coat with seasoning mix.
2. Cover, cook on low for 12 hours. Remove the beef brisket from the liquid, place it on a pan. Sear it under the broiler for 2-4 minutes, observe it, so the meat doesn't burn. Cover it with foil, let it rest within 1 hour. Slice and serve.

Nutrition: Calories: 280 Carbs: 4g Fat: 20g Protein: 20g

38. Seriously Delicious Lamb Roast

Preparation time: 15 minutes
Cooking time: 8 hours
Servings: 8

Ingredients:
- 12 medium radishes, scrubbed, washed, and cut in half
- Salt and pepper to taste
- 1 red onion, diced
- 2 garlic cloves, minced
- 1 lamb joint (approximately 4.5 pounds) at room temperature
- 2 Tablespoons olive oil
- 1 teaspoon dry oregano
- 1 teaspoon dry thyme
- 1 sprig fresh rosemary
- 4 cups heated broth, your choice

Directions:
1. Place cut radishes along the bottom of the crockpot. Season. Add onion and garlic. Mix the herbs plus olive oil in a small bowl. Mix until a paste develops.
2. Place the meat on top of the radishes. Massage the paste over the surface of the meat. Heat the stock,

pour it around the meat. Cover, cook on low for 8 hours. Let it rest for 20 minutes. Slice and serve.

Nutrition: Calories: 206 Carbs: 4g Fat: 9g Protein: 32g

39. Dressed Pork Leg Roast

Preparation time: 15 minutes
Cooking time: 8 hours
Servings: 14

Ingredients:
- 8 pounds pork leg
- 1 Tablespoon butter
- 1 yellow onion, sliced
- 6 garlic cloves, peeled and minced
- 2 Tablespoons ground cumin
- 2 Tablespoons ground thyme
- 2 Tablespoons ground chili
- 1 teaspoon salt
- 1 teaspoon fresh ground black pepper
- 1 cup hot water

Directions:
1. Butter the crockpot. Slice crisscrosses along the top of pork leg. Arrange onion slices and minced garlic along the bottom of the crockpot.
2. Place meat on top of vegetables. In a small bowl, mix the herbs. Rub it all over the pork leg. Add the water. Cover, cook on high for 8 hours. Remove from crockpot, place on a platter, cover with foil. Let it rest for 1 hour. Shred the meat and serve.

Nutrition: Calories: 179 Carbs: 0g Fat: 8g Protein: 25g

40. Rabbit & Mushroom Stew

Preparation time: 15 minutes
Cooking time: 6 hours
Servings: 6

Ingredients:
- 1 rabbit, in portion size pieces
- 2 cups spicy Spanish sausage, cut into chunks
- 2 Tablespoons butter, divided
- 1 red onion, sliced
- 1 cup button mushrooms, washed and dried
- 1 teaspoon cayenne pepper
- 1 teaspoon sweet paprika
- 1 teaspoon salt
- 1 teaspoon fresh ground black pepper
- 1 cup chicken broth+1 cup hot water

Directions:
1. Butter the crockpot. In a large pan, melt the butter, add the rabbit pieces, brown on all sides. Transfer to crockpot.
2. In the same pan, sauté the onions, sausage chunks, and spices for 2-3 minutes. Put in chicken broth,

heat on high for 1 minute, then pour the mixture over the rabbit.

3. Add the mushrooms. Adjust the seasoning if needed. Add the water. Cover, cook on high for 6 hours. Serve.

Nutrition: Calories: 189 Carbs: 20g Fat: 6g Protein: 13g

41. Italian Spicy Sausage & Bell Peppers

Preparation time: 15 minutes
Cooking time: 6 hours
Servings: 5
Ingredients:
- 2 Tablespoons butter
- 2 red onions, sliced
- 4 bell peppers, sliced
- 2 regular cans Italian tomatoes, diced
  - pounds spicy Italian sausage
- 1 teaspoon dry oregano
- 1 teaspoon dry thyme
- 1 teaspoon dry basil
- 1 teaspoon sweet paprika
- 1 teaspoon salt
- 1 teaspoon fresh ground black pepper

Directions:
1. Butter the crockpot. Add the sliced onions, peppers, and salt. Pour the tomatoes over them. Toss well.
2. Add seasoning. Mix it in. Arrange sausages in the middle of the pepper and onion mixture. Add ¼ cup hot water. Cover, cook on low for 6 hours. Serve.

Nutrition: Calories: 320 Carbs: 15g Fat: 17g Protein: 28g

42. Chicken in Salsa Verde

Preparation time: 15 minutes
Cooking time: 6 hours
Servings: 4
Ingredients:
  - pounds of chicken breasts
- 3 bunches parsley, chopped
- ¾ cup olive oil
- ¼ cup capers, drained and chopped
- 3 anchovy fillets
- 1 lemon, juice, and zest
- 2 garlic cloves, minced
- 1 teaspoon salt
- 1 teaspoon fresh ground black pepper

Directions:
1. Place the chicken breasts in the crockpot. Mix the rest of the fixing in a blender, pour over the chicken. Cover, cook on low for 6 hours. Shred with a fork and serve.

Nutrition: Calories: 145 Carbs: 5g Fat: 2g Protein: 26g

43.

44. Salmon Poached in White Wine and Lemon

Preparation time: 15 minutes
Cooking time: 2 hours
Servings: 4

Ingredients:
- 2 cups of water
- 1 cup cooking wine, white
- 1 lemon, sliced thin
- 1 small mild onion, sliced thin
- 1 bay leaf
- 1 mixed bunch fresh tarragon, dill, and parsley
- 1 kg salmon fillet, skin on
- 1 teaspoon salt
- 1 teaspoon ground black pepper

Directions:
1. Add all ingredients, except salmon and seasoning, to the crockpot. Cover, cook on low for 1 hour. Season the salmon, place in the crockpot skin-side down. Cover, cook on low for another hour. Serve.

Nutrition: Calories: 216 Carbs: 1g Fat: 12g Protein: 23g

45. Beef and Onion Crock Pot

Preparation time: 15 minutes
Cooking time: 9 hours
Servings: 6

Ingredients:
- 2 lbs. lean beef, cut into cubes
- 2 lbs. shallots, peeled
- 2-3 garlic cloves, peeled, whole
- 3 tbsp. tomato paste, dissolved in 1/2 cup water
- 2 cups chicken broth
- 2 bay leaves
- 4 tbsp. red wine vinegar
- 1 tsp salt

Directions:
1. Combine all ingredients in crockpot. Cover and cook on low within 7-9 hours.

Nutrition: Calories: 214 Carbs: 12g Fat: 6g Protein: 27g

46. Beef and Green Pea Crock Pot

Preparation time: 15 minutes
Cooking time: 9 hours
Servings: 6

Ingredients:
- 2 lbs. stewing beef
- 2 bags of frozen peas
- 1 onion, chopped
- 2 carrots, chopped
- 3-4 garlic cloves, cut
- 2 cups chicken broth
- 1 tsp salt
- 1 tbsp. paprika
- 1/2 cup fresh dill, finely chopped
- 1 cup yogurt, to serve

Directions:
1. Combine all the fixing listed in crockpot. Cover and cook on low within 7-9 hours. Serve sprinkled with dill and a dollop of yogurt.

Nutrition: Calories: 391 Carbs: 31g Fat: 16g Protein: 29g

47. Beef and Root Vegetable Crock Pot

Preparation time: 15 minutes
Cooking time: 9 hours
Servings: 6

Ingredients:
- 2 lbs. stewing beef
- 2 carrots, cut
- 2 onions, sliced
- 1 turnip, peeled and diced
- 1 beet, peeled and diced
- 1-2 parsnips, diced
- 2 cups beef broth
- 1 tbsp. tomato paste
- 1 tbsp. paprika
- 2 bay leaves

Directions:
1. Combine all ingredients in crockpot. Cover and cook on low within 7-9 hours. Serve.

Nutrition: Calories: 232 Carbs: 12g Fat: 15g Protein: 12g

48. Slow Cooked Mediterranean Beef

Preparation time: 15 minutes
Cooking time: 9 hours
Servings: 6

Ingredients:
- 2 lbs. lean steak, cut into large pieces
- 2 onions, sliced
- 2-3 garlic cloves, whole
- 1 green pepper, cut
- 1/2 bag frozen green beans
- 1/2 bag frozen green peas
- 1/2 frozen bag okra
- 1 zucchini, peeled and cut
- 1 small eggplant, peeled and diced
- 1 tomato, diced
- 2 tbsp. tomato paste or purée
- 1 cup chicken broth
- 1 tsp dried oregano
- salt and black pepper, to taste

Directions:
1. Combine all ingredients in crockpot. Cover and cook on low within 7-9 hours.

Nutrition: Calories: 156 Carbs: 8g Fat: 5g Protein: 19g

50. <u>Slow Cooker Paprika Chicken</u>

Preparation time: 15 minutes
Cooking time: 6 hours
Servings: 4

Ingredients:
- 8 chicken drumsticks or 4 breast halves
- 1 onion, chopped
- 3 slices bacon, finely chopped
- 1 large red pepper, chopped
- 1 large green pepper, chopped
- 2-3 garlic cloves, finely chopped
- 1 tbsp. paprika
- 1 can of crushed tomatoes
- 2 cups chicken broth
- 1/3 cup medium-grain white rice
- 1 tbsp. sour cream
- 1 cup fresh parsley, finely cut, to serve

Directions:
1. Combine all ingredients in a slow cooker. Cover and cook on low within 5-6 hours.

Nutrition: Calories: 484 Carbs: 6g Fat: 32g Protein: 42g

51. <u>Slow Cooked Lamb with Red Wine Sauce</u>

Preparation time: 15 minutes
Cooking time: 7 hours
Servings: 4

Ingredients:
- 4 trimmed lamb shanks
- 1 onion, thinly sliced
- 2 large carrots, roughly chopped
- 2-3 parsnips, roughly chopped
- 1 cup chicken broth
- 2 cups dry red wine
- 1 tsp brown sugar
- ½ tsp black pepper
- ½ tsp salt

Directions:
1. Spray the slow cooker with nonstick spray. Place the lamb shanks in it with all other ingredients. Cover and cook on low for 6-7 hours.

Nutrition: Calories: 736 Carbs: 4g Fat: 41g Protein: 17g

52. <u>Pork and Mushroom Crock Pot</u>

Preparation time: 15 minutes
Cooking time: 9 hours
Servings: 4

Ingredients:
- 2 lbs. pork tenderloin, sliced
- 1 lb. chopped white button mushrooms
- 1 can cream of mushroom soup
- 1 cup sour cream
- salt and black pepper, to taste

Directions:
1. Spray the slow cooker with nonstick spray. Combine all ingredients into the slow cooker. Cover, and cook on low within 7-9 hours.

Nutrition: Calories: 275 Carbs: 33g Fat: 7g Protein: 21g

53. <u>Slow Cooked Pot Roast</u>

Preparation time: 15 minutes
Cooking time: 10 hours
Servings: 4

Ingredients:
- 2 lb. pot roast
- 1-2 garlic cloves, crushed
- 1 small onion, finely cut
- 1/3 cup tomato paste
- 1/2 cup chicken broth
- 2 tbsp. Worcestershire sauce
- salt, to taste

Directions:
1. Spray the slow cooker with nonstick spray. Place the roast in the slow cooker. In a bowl, combine the tomato paste, chicken broth, Worcestershire sauce, garlic, and onions. Spread this sauce over the meat. Cook on low within 8-10 hours.

Nutrition: Calories: 340 Carbs: 46g Fat: 4g Protein: 29g

55. Slow-Cooked Mediterranean Pork Casserole

Preparation time: 15 minutes
Cooking time: 10 hours
Servings: 4
Ingredients:

- 2 lbs. pork loin, cut into cubes
- 1 large onion, chopped
- 2 cups white button mushrooms, cut
- 1-2 garlic cloves, finely chopped
- 1 green pepper, cut into strips
- 1 red pepper, cut into strips
- 1 small eggplant, peeled and diced
- 1 zucchini, peeled and diced
- 2 tomatoes, diced
- 1 cup chicken broth
- 1/2 tsp cumin
- 1 tbsp. paprika
- salt and black pepper, to taste

Directions:

1. Spray the slow cooker with nonstick spray. Place the pork in the slow cooker. Put in all other fixings and stir to combine. Cook on low within 8-10 hours.

Nutrition: Calories: 265 Carbs: 0g Fat: 9g Protein: 0g

56. Pizza Ravioli Mix Up

Preparation time: 15 minutes
Cooking time: 3 hours
Servings: 12
Ingredients:

- 1 1/2 lb. ground beef round
- 1 1/2 lb. bulk Italian pork sausage
- 2 medium onions, chopped
- 2 tablespoons finely chopped garlic
- 2 jars tomato pasta sauce
- 1 bag frozen cheese-filled ravioli
- 3 cups Cheddar-Monterey Jack cheese blend, shredded
- 1 package sliced pepperoni
- 1/4 cup sliced ripe olives
- Fresh basil sprigs, if desired

Directions:

1. Grease the bottom of 5- to 6-quart your slow cooker using cooking spray. Arrange side of your slow cooker with foil; spray it with cooking spray.
2. Cook sausage over medium heat within 8 to 10 minutes in a 12-inch skillet, then drain it after. Put the sausage in a bowl.
3. Cook the beef, onion plus garlic over medium heat 8 to 10 minutes in the same skillet, drain. Mix the

beef mixture plus 1 jar of the pasta sauce to the bowl with sausage.
4. Spread half of the rest of the jar of pasta sauce to cover the bottom in a slow cooker. Arrange with half of the ravioli and half of the meat mixture.
5. Sprinkle with 1 1/2 cups of the cheese and half of the pepperoni. Repeat layers. Cook on low within 3 hours. Sprinkle with olives before serving. Garnish with basil.

Nutrition: Calories: 140 Carbs: 20g Fat: 5g Protein: 4g

57. Chicken Cacciatore with Linguine

Preparation time: 15 minutes
Cooking time: 10 hours & 10 minutes
Servings: 6
Ingredients:

- 2 1/2 lb. boneless skinless chicken thighs
- 1 jar sliced mushrooms, drained
- 2 cans Italian-style tomato paste
- 1 3/4 cups chicken broth
- 1/2 cup white wine, if desired
- 1 1/2 teaspoons dried basil leaves
- 1/2 teaspoon salt
- 1 dried bay leaf
- 12 oz. uncooked linguine
- 1/4 teaspoon dried thyme leaves
- 1 tablespoon cornstarch
- Shredded Parmesan cheese, if desired

Directions:

1. Grease 3- to 4-quart slow cooker using a cooking spray. Put the chicken in the cooker. Put the mushrooms, tomato paste, broth, wine, basil, salt, and bay leaf; gently stir to mix.
2. Cover then cook on Low heat within 8 to 10 hours. Before serving, cook then drain linguine.
3. Remove and cover to keep warm. Mix the thyme into the sauce in the cooker. Increase heat setting to High. In a small bowl, mix 1/4 cup sauce from the cooker and the cornstarch until smooth.
4. Cook 10 minutes longer, stirring frequently. Remove bay leaf before serving. Serve chicken and sauce over linguine. Sprinkle with cheese.

Nutrition: Calories: 180 Carbs: 26g Fat: 3g Protein: 12g

59. Italian Steak Roll

Preparation time: 15 minutes
Cooking time: 6 hours
Servings: 2

Ingredients:

- 3/4 lb. beef round steak (1/2-inch-thick), trimmed of fat
- 1/2 tsp dried Italian seasoning
- 1/4 tsp salt
- 1/4 tsp pepper
- 1 thin slice onion, halved
- 1 clove garlic, minced
- 1/2 cup mushrooms, sliced
- 1 medium sliced Italian plum tomato, cut into quarters
- 3/4 cup savory beef gravy

Directions:

1. Put the steak on your work surface, rub with Italian seasoning, salt plus pepper. Put the onion slice halves, then roll up the beef, with onion inside; tie with string.
2. Put the beef roll, seam side down, in 2- to 3-quart slow cooker. Sprinkle garlic, mushrooms, and tomato around the roll. Spoon gravy over the roll.
3. Cook on low within 5 to 6 hours. Remove then put it on serving platter. Remove the string, then slice the beef roll. Mix in the gravy batter in your slow cooker until blended. Serve beef roll slices with gravy.

Nutrition: Calories: 190 Carbs: 37g Fat: 2g Protein: 6g

60. Chicken Parmesan with Penne Pasta

Preparation time: 15 minutes
Cooking time: 6 hours
Servings: 4

Ingredients:

- 1 egg
- 1/3 cup plain bread crumbs
- 1/3 cup shredded Parmesan cheese
- 1/2 tsp Italian seasoning
- 1/4 tsp salt
- 1/4 tsp pepper
- 4 boneless skinless chicken breasts
- 1 jar tomato pasta sauce
- 1/2 cup shredded Italian cheese blend
- 2 & 2/3 cups uncooked penne pasta

Directions:

1. Grease your 2- to 3-quart slow cooker using a cooking spray. Beat egg until foamy in a small shallow bowl. Mix the bread crumbs, Parmesan cheese, Italian seasoning, salt plus pepper in a separate shallow bowl.
2. Soak the chicken into egg, then to bread crumb mixture; place in cooker. Spread pasta sauce evenly over chicken. Cover; cook on Low heat within 5 to 6 hours.
3. Sprinkle it with Italian cheese blend on top. Cook on low within 10 minutes longer. Cook your pasta following what stated on the package directions. Serve chicken with pasta.

Nutrition: Calories: 170 Carbs: 15g Fat: 5g Protein: 17g

61. Chicken Cacciatore

Preparation time: 15 minutes
Cooking time: 9 hours
Servings: 6

Ingredients:

- 6 skinless, boneless chicken breast halves
- 1 (28 ounces) jar spaghetti sauce
- 2 green bell pepper, seeded and cubed
- 8 ounces fresh mushrooms, sliced
- 1 onion, finely diced
- 2 tablespoons minced garlic

Directions:

1. Put the chicken in your slow cooker, then the spaghetti sauce, green bell peppers, mushrooms, onion, plus garlic. Cook on low within 7 to 9 hours.

Nutrition: Calories: 210 Carbs: 9g Fat: 3g Protein: 26g

62. Lasagna

Preparation time: 15 minutes
Cooking time: 6 hours
Servings: 10

Ingredients:

- 1-pound lean ground beef
- 1 onion, chopped
- 2 teaspoons minced garlic
- 1 (29 ounces) can tomato sauce
- 1 (6 ounces) can tomato paste
- 1 1/2 teaspoons salt
- 1 teaspoon dried oregano
- 1 package of lasagna noodles
- 12 oz. cottage cheese
- 1/2 cup grated Parmesan cheese
- 16 oz. shredded mozzarella cheese

Directions:

1. Cook the onion, garlic, and ground beef until brown in a large skillet over medium heat. Put the tomato sauce, tomato paste, salt, and oregano and

stir until well incorporated. Cook until heated through.

2. Mix the cottage cheese, grated Parmesan cheese, plus shredded mozzarella cheese in a large bowl. Put a layer of the meat batters into the bottom of your slow cooker. Put a double layer of the uncooked lasagna noodles.

3. Top it with a portion of the cheese mixture. Repeat the layering of sauce, noodles, and cheese until all the ingredients are used. Cook on LOW within 4 to 6 hours.

Nutrition: Calories: 275 Carbs: 42g Fat: 3g Protein: 15g

63. Cheesy Italian Tortellini

Preparation time: 15 minutes
Cooking time: 8 hours
Servings: 6

Ingredients:
*   1/2-pound ground beef
*   1/2-pound Italian sausage
*   1 jar marinara sauce
*   1 can sliced mushrooms
*   1 can Italian-style diced tomatoes, undrained
*   1 package refrigerated or fresh cheese tortellini
*   1 cup mozzarella cheese, shredded
*   1/2 cup Cheddar cheese, shredded

Directions:
1. Cook the ground beef plus Italian sausage into a large skillet over medium-high heat until browned, then drain. Mix the ground meats, marinara sauce, mushrooms, plus tomatoes in your slow cooker. Cook on LOW within 7 to 8 hours.

2. Mix in the tortellini, plus sprinkle the mozzarella, then the cheddar cheese over the top. Cook within 15 more minutes on LOW.

Nutrition: Calories: 331 Carbs: 24g Fat: 16g Protein: 22g

64. Easy Meatballs

Preparation time: 15 minutes
Cooking time: 8 hours
Servings: 16

Ingredients:
*   1 & 1/4 cups Italian seasoned bread crumbs
*   & 1/2-pounds ground beef
*   2 cloves garlic, minced
*   1/4 cup chopped fresh parsley
*   1 medium yellow onion, chopped
*   1 egg, beaten
*   1 jar spaghetti sauce

*   1 can of crushed tomatoes
*   1 can tomato puree

Directions:
1. Mix the ground beef, bread crumbs, parsley, garlic, onion, and egg in a bowl. Shape the mixture into 16 meatballs.

2. In a slow cooker, mix the spaghetti sauce, crushed tomatoes, and tomato puree. Place the meatballs into the sauce mixture. Cook on low within 6 to 8 hours.

Nutrition: Calories: 280 Carbs: 13g Fat: 15g Protein: 24g

65. Chicken Alfredo

Preparation time: 15 minutes
Cooking time: 5 hours
Servings: 4

Ingredients:
*   4 skinless, boneless chicken breast halves
*   1/4 cup water
*   1 package dry Italian-style salad dressing mix
*   1 clove garlic, pressed
*   1 package cream cheese, softened
*   1 can condensed cream of chicken soup
*   1 can chop canned mushrooms
*   1 package spaghetti
*   1 tablespoon chopped fresh parsley
*   Cooking spray

Directions:
1. Grease the crock of your slow cooker using a nonstick cooking spray. Place chicken breasts in the crock. Mix the Italian dressing and water in a small bowl and pour over chicken. Rub the chicken with garlic, then cook on low within 4 hours.

2. Mix softened cream cheese plus cream of chicken soup in a bowl. Put on chicken, then stir in mushrooms. Cook on low within 1 additional hour.

3. Fill with lightly salted water in a large pot and boil over high heat. Stir in the spaghetti, then return to a boil.

4. Cook the pasta uncovered, occasionally stirring, within 12 minutes, then drain. Before you serve, scoop chicken plus sauce on hot cooked pasta, then sprinkle with parsley.

Nutrition: Calories: 280 Carbs: 21g Fat: 16g Protein: 13g

67. Pork Cacciatore

Preparation time: 15 minutes
Cooking time: 8 hours
Servings: 4

Ingredients:
- 2 tbsp. olive oil
- 1 sliced onion
- 4 boneless pork chops
- 1 jar pasta sauce
- 1 can diced tomatoes
- 1 green bell pepper, strips
- 1 package fresh mushrooms, sliced
- 2 large cloves garlic, minced
- 1 tsp Italian seasoning
- 1/2 tsp dried basil
- 1/2 cup dry white wine
- 4 slices mozzarella cheese

Directions:
1. Cook the pork chops over medium-high heat in a large skillet, then transfer it to your slow cooker. Cook onion in oil on medium heat in the same pan. Mix in mushrooms plus bell pepper until they are soft.
2. Mix in pasta sauce, diced tomatoes, plus white wine. Season with Italian seasoning, basil, and garlic. Pour over pork chops in the slow cooker. Cook on low within 7 to 8 hours. Put cheese slices on each chop and cover with sauce to serve.

Nutrition: Calories: 252 Carbs: 23g Fat: 6g Protein: 26g

68. Italian Beef Roast

Preparation time: 15 minutes
Cooking time: 8 hours
Servings: 8

Ingredients:
- 1 beef chuck roast
- 1 quartered onion
- 1 can beef broth
- 1 packet dry au jus mix
- 1 package dry Italian salad dressing mix
- 1/2 teaspoon salt
- 1/2 teaspoon ground black pepper

Directions:
1. Put the beef chuck roast into your slow cooker, then scatter onion quarters around the meat. Put the beef broth on the meat, then sprinkle the au jus mix, Italian salad dressing mix, salt, plus black pepper over the roast. Set on low within 6 to 8 hours.

Nutrition: Calories: 60 Carbs: 1g Fat: 2g Protein: 11g

69. Rosemary and Red Pepper Chicken

Preparation time: 15 minutes
Cooking time: 7 hours
Servings: 8

Ingredients:
- 1 thinly sliced small onion
- 1 medium red bell pepper, thinly sliced
- 4 cloves garlic, minced
- 2 teaspoons dried rosemary
- 1/2 teaspoon dried oregano
- 8 ounces Italian turkey sausages, casings removed
- 8 skinless, boneless chicken breast halves
- 1/4 teaspoon coarsely ground pepper
- 1/4 cup dry vermouth
- 1 1/2 tablespoons cornstarch
- 2 tablespoons cold water
- Salt to taste
- 1/4 cup chopped fresh parsley

Directions:
2. In a 5 to 6-quart slow cooker, mix onion, bell pepper, garlic, rosemary, plus oregano. Put the sausages over the onion mixture. Rinse chicken, then pat dry; arrange in a single layer on the sausage.
3. Put pepper, then pour in vermouth. Cook on low within 5 to 7 hours. Stir cornstarch plus cold water in a small bowl. Mix into cooking liquid in your slow cooker. Adjust the heat to high, stirring within 2 to 3 times, until sauce is thickened. Serve with a sprinkle of parsley.

Nutrition: Calories: 130 Carbs: 13g Fat: 7g Protein: 4g

70. Braciole

Preparation time: 15 minutes
Cooking time: 8 hours
Servings: 6

Ingredients:
- 2 jars marinara sauce
- 2 beaten eggs
- 1/2 cup dry bread crumbs
- 1 flank steak, pounded
- 1 tsp kosher salt
- Ground black pepper
- 5 bacon slices
- 1 cup Italian cheese blend, shredded
- 2 tbsp. vegetable oil

Directions:

1. Put the marinara sauce into your slow cooker and set it on High to warm. Mix the eggs plus the breadcrumbs in a bowl. Rub each side of the meat with salt plus pepper.
2. Pat the breadcrumb batter over one side of the flank steak, leaving about a one-inch border around the edges. Top it with the bacon slices, then with shredded cheese. Beginning from one long side, roll flank steak into a log, then use toothpicks to secure the log.
3. Warm the oil in a heavy skillet. Cook the stuffed flank steak in the hot oil within 10 minutes, then transfer it to the warm sauce in your slow cooker. Put the sauce on meat to cover. Cook on low within 6 to 8 hours. Remove the toothpicks before slicing. Serve with marinara.

Nutrition: Calories: 137 Carbs: 0g Fat: 5g Protein: 23g

71. Eggplant Parmesan

Preparation time: 15 minutes
Cooking time: 5 hours
Servings: 8

Ingredients:

- 4 eggplant, sliced
- 1 tbsp. salt
- 1 cup extra-virgin olive oil
- 2 eggs
- 1/3 cup water
- 3 tbsp. all-purpose flour
- 1/3 cup seasoned bread crumbs
- 1/2 cup Parmesan cheese, grated
- 1 jar prepared marinara sauce
- 1 package mozzarella cheese, sliced

Directions:

1. Put the eggplant slices in a bowl in layers, sprinkle it with salt. Let stand for 30 minutes to drain. Rinse and dry on paper towels.
2. Warm-up olive oil in a skillet on medium heat. Mix the eggs with water plus flour. Soak the eggplant

Nutrition: Calories: 240 Carbs: 23g Fat: 9g Protein: 15g

slices in batter, then fry in the hot oil until golden brown. Mix the seasoned bread crumbs with Parmesan cheese in a bowl.

3. Put 1/4 of the eggplant slices into your crockpot, then top with 1/4 of the crumbs, 1/4 of the marinara sauce, plus 1/4 of the mozzarella cheese. Repeat layers three more times. Cook on low within 4 to 5 hours.

Nutrition: Calories: 271 Carbs: 21g Fat: 17g Protein: 9g

72. Ravioli Lasagna

Preparation time: 15 minutes
Cooking time: 6 hours
Servings: 8

Ingredients:

- 1-pound ground beef
- 1 tbsp. chopped garlic
- 1 tsp garlic powder
- 1 tsp salt
- 1/2 tsp ground black pepper
- 2 jars prepared pasta sauce
- 1 tsp Italian seasoning
- 1 tsp dried basil
- 1 tsp dried oregano
- 1 package cheese ravioli
- 2 cups mozzarella cheese, shredded

Directions:

1. Warm a large skillet on medium-high heat. Cook the beef, garlic, garlic powder, salt, plus pepper in the hot skillet within 5 to 7 minutes.
2. Drain and discard all the grease, then mix in pasta sauce, Italian seasoning, basil, plus oregano into the ground beef batter.
3. Put a layer of meat sauce into your slow cooker, then put a layer of ravioli. Put another layer of meat sauce on the ravioli layer; alternate.
4. Cook on low within 3 to 5 hours. Put the ravioli mixture with mozzarella cheese and cook again within 45 minutes to 1 hour more.

73. Sauerkraut

Preparation time: 15 minutes
Cooking time: 8 hours
Servings: 6

Ingredients:
- 2 pounds of sauerkraut, drained
- 2 tablespoons bacon drops
- 2 onion, coarsely chopped
- 1 1/4 cup beef broth
- 3 whole cloves
- 1 bay leaf
- 4 juniper berries
- 2 teaspoons caraway seed
- salt to taste
- 1 tsp of white sugar, or to taste

Directions:
1. Put the sauerkraut, bacon drops, and onion in a slow cooker. Put in the beef broth, then season with cloves, bay leaves, juniper berries, caraway seeds, salt, and sugar. Stir to combine. Cook on Low 8 hours.

Nutrition: Calories 111 Fat 5.2 g Carbohydrates 14.9 g Protein 3 g

74. Refried Beans without the Refry

Preparation time: 15 minutes
Cooking time: 8 hours
Servings: 15

Ingredients:
- 1 onion, peeled and halved
- 3 cups of dry pinto beans, rinsed
- 1/2 fresh jalapeno pepper, without seeds and minced meat
- 2 tablespoons chopped garlic
- 5 teaspoons of salt
- 1 3/4 teaspoons of freshly ground black pepper
- 1/8 teaspoon ground cumin, optional
- 9 cups of water

Directions:
1. Put the onion, rinsed beans, jalapeno, garlic, salt, pepper, and cumin in a slow cooker. Put in the water and mix to combine. Boil for 8 hours on High and add more water if necessary.
2. When the beans are done, sift them and save the liquid. Puree the beans with a potato masher and add the reserved water if necessary to achieve the desired consistency.

Nutrition: Calories 139 Fat 0.5 g Carbohydrates 25.4 g Protein 8.5 g

75. Spicy Black-Eyed Peas

Preparation time: 15 minutes
Cooking time: 6 hours
Servings: 10

Ingredients:
- 6 cups of water
- 1 cube chicken broth
- 1 pound of dried peas with black eyes, sorted and rinsed
- 1 onion, diced
- 2 cloves of garlic, diced
- 1 red pepper, stemmed, seeded, and diced
- 1 jalapeno Chili, without seeds and minced meat
- 8 grams diced ham
- 4 slices of bacon, minced meat
- 1/2 teaspoon cayenne pepper
- 1 1/2 teaspoon of cumin
- salt
- 1 tsp ground black pepper

Directions:
1. Put the water into your slow cooker, add the stock cube, and stir to dissolve. Combine the peas with black eyes, onion, garlic, bell pepper, jalapeno pepper, ham, bacon, cayenne pepper, cumin, salt, and pepper; stir to mix. Cover the slow cooker and cook for 6 to 8 hours on low until the beans are soft.

Nutrition: Calories 199 Fat 2.9 g Carbohydrates 30.2 g Protein 14.1 g

76. Sweet Potato Casserole

Preparation time: 15 minutes
Cooking time: 4 hours
Servings: 8

Ingredients:
- 2 (29 ounces) cans of sweet potatoes, drained and mashed
- 1/3 cup butter, melted
- 2 tablespoons white sugar
- 2 tablespoons brown sugar
- 1 tablespoon orange juice
- 2 eggs, beaten
- 1/2 cup of milk
- 1/3 cup chopped pecans
- 1/3 cup of brown sugar
- 2 tablespoons all-purpose flour
- 2 teaspoons butter, melted

Directions:
1. Lightly grease a slow cooker. Mix sweet potatoes, 1/3 cup butter, white sugar, and 2 tablespoons brown sugar in a large bowl. Add orange juice, eggs, and milk. Transfer it to the prepared oven dish.
2. Mix the pecans, 1/3 cup brown sugar, flour plus 2 tablespoons butter in a small bowl. Spread the mixture over the sweet potatoes. Cover the slow cooker and cook for 3 to 4 hours on HIGH.

Nutrition: Calories 406 Fat 13.8 g Carbohydrates 66.1 g Protein 6.3 g

77. Baked Potatoes

Preparation time: 15 minutes
Cooking time: 4 hours & 30 minutes
Servings: 4

Ingredients:
- Bake 4 potatoes, scrubbed well
- 1 tablespoon extra-virgin olive oil
- kosher salt to taste
- 4 sheets of aluminum foil

Directions:
1. Prick the potatoes all over, then massage the potatoes with olive oil, sprinkle with salt, and wrap them firmly in foil. Put the potatoes in a slow cooker, cook for 4 1/2 to 5 hours on High, or 7 1/2 to 8 hours on low until cooked.

Nutrition: Calories 254 Fat 3.6 g Carbohydrates 51.2 g Protein 6.1 g

78. Slow Cooker Stuffing

Preparation time: 15 minutes
Cooking time: 8 hours
Servings: 4

Ingredients:
- 1 cup of butter or margarine
- 2 cups chopped onion
- 2 cups chopped celery
- 1/4 cup chopped fresh parsley
- 12 grams of sliced mushrooms
- 12 cups of dry bread cubes
- 1 teaspoon seasoning for poultry
- 1 1/2 teaspoons dried sage
- 1 teaspoon dried thyme
- 1/2 teaspoon dried marjoram
- 1 1/2 teaspoons of salt
- 1/2 teaspoon ground black pepper
- 4 & 1/2 cups of chicken broth
- 2 eggs, beaten

Directions:
2. Dissolve the butter or margarine in a frying pan over medium heat. Cook onion, celery, mushroom, and parsley in butter, stirring regularly.
3. Put boiled vegetables over bread cubes in a huge mixing bowl. Season with poultry herbs, sage, thyme, marjoram, and salt and pepper.
4. Pour enough broth to moisten and mix the eggs. Transfer the mixture to the slow cooker and cover. Bake 45 minutes on High, turn the heat to low, and cook for 4 to 8 hours.

Nutrition: Calories 197 Fat 13.1 g Carbohydrates 16.6 g Protein 3.9 g

79. Slow Cooker Mashed Potatoes

Preparation time: 15 minutes
Cooking time: 3 hours & 15 minutes
Servings: 8

Ingredients:
- 5 pounds of red potatoes, cut into pieces
- 1 tablespoon minced garlic, or to taste
- 3 cubes of chicken broth
- 1 (8 ounces) container of sour cream
- 1 package of cream cheese, softened
- 1/2 cup butter
- salt and pepper to taste

Directions:
1. Boil the potatoes, garlic, and broth in a large pan with lightly salted boiling water until soft but firm, about 15 minutes.
2. Drain, reserve water. Mashed potatoes in a bowl with sour cream and cream cheese; add reserved

water if necessary to achieve the desired consistency.

3. Transfer it to your slow cooker, cook for 2 to 3 hours on low. Stir in butter just before serving and season with salt and pepper.

Nutrition: Calories 470 Fat 27.7 g Carbohydrates 47.9 g Protein 8.8 g

80. <u>Scalloped Potatoes with Ham</u>

Preparation time: 15 minutes
Cooking time: 4 hours
Servings: 8
Ingredients:

- 3 pounds of potatoes, thin slices
- 1 cup grated Cheddar cheese
- 1/2 cup chopped onion
- 1 cup chopped cooked ham
- 1 can of condensed mushroom soup
- 1/2 cup of water
- 1/2 teaspoon of garlic powder
- 1/4 teaspoon of salt
- 1/4 teaspoon of black pepper

Directions:

1. Place sliced potatoes in a slow cooker. Mix the grated cheese, onion, and ham in a medium bowl. Mix with potatoes in a slow cooker.
2. Use the same bowl and mix condensed soup and water. Season with garlic powder, salt, and pepper. Pour evenly over the potato mixture. Cook on High within 4 hours.

Nutrition: Calories 265 Fat 10.2 g Carbohydrates 33.3 g Protein 10.8 g

81. <u>Classic Coney Sauce</u>

Preparation time: 15 minutes
Cooking time: 2 hours
Servings: 12
Ingredients:

- 2 pounds of ground beef
- 1/2 cup chopped onion
- 1 1/2 cups of ketchup
- 1/4 cup of white sugar
- 1/4 cup white vinegar
- 1/4 cup prepared yellow mustard
- 1/2 teaspoon celery seed
- 3/4 teaspoon Worcestershire sauce
- 1/2 teaspoon ground black pepper
- 3/4 teaspoon of salt

Directions:

1. Place the minced meat and onion in a large frying pan over medium-high heat. Cook, stirring, until the meat is brown. Drain.

2. Transfer the steak plus onion to your slow cooker, then mix in the ketchup, sugar, vinegar, plus mustard. Put the celery seed, Worcestershire sauce, pepper plus salt. Simmer on low within a few hours before you serve.

Nutrition: Calories 186 Fat 9.2 g Carbohydrates 12.8 g Protein 13.5 g

82. <u>Spiced Slow Cooker Applesauce</u>

Preparation time: 15 minutes
Cooking time: 6 hours & 30 minutes
Servings: 8
Ingredients:

- 8 apples - peeled, without the core and cut into thin slices
- 1/2 cup of water
- 3/4 cup packaged brown sugar
- 1/2 teaspoon pumpkin pie spice

Directions:

1. Mix the apples plus water in your slow cooker; cook on low within 6 to 8 hours. Mix in the brown sugar plus pumpkin pie spice; continue cooking for another 30 minutes.

Nutrition: Calories 150 Fat 0.2 g Carbohydrates 39.4 g Protein 0.4 g

83. <u>Homemade Beans</u>

Preparation time: 15 minutes
Cooking time: 10 hours
Servings: 12

Ingredients:

- 3 cups of dried navy beans, soaked overnight or cooked for an hour
- 1 1/2 cups of ketchup
- 1 1/2 cups of water
- 1/4 cup molasses
- 1 large onion, minced
- 1 tablespoon dry mustard
- 1 tablespoon of salt
- 6 thick-sliced bacon, cut into 1-inch pieces
- 1 cup of brown sugar

Directions:

1. Pour soaking liquid from beans and place in a slow cooker. Stir ketchup, water, molasses, onion, mustard, salt, bacon, and brown sugar through the beans until everything is well mixed. Cook on LOW within 8 to 10 hours, occasionally stirring if possible, although not necessary.

Nutrition: Calories 296 Fat 3 g Carbohydrates 57 g Protein 12.4 g

84. Western Omelet

Preparation time: 15 minutes
Cooking time: 12 hours
Servings: 12
Ingredients:
- 1 (2 pounds) package of frozen grated hashish brown potatoes
- 1 pound diced cooked ham
- 1 onion, diced
- 1 green pepper, seeded and diced
- 1 1/2 cups grated cheddar cheese
- 12 eggs
- 1 cup of milk
- salt and pepper to taste

Directions:
1. Grease a slow cooker of 4 liters or larger in light. Layer 1/3 of the mashed potatoes in a layer on the bottom.
2. Layer 1/3 of the ham, onion, green pepper, and cheddar cheese. Repeat layers two more times. Whisk the eggs plus milk in a large bowl and season with salt and pepper. Put over the contents of the slow cooker. Cook on low within 10 to 12 hours.

Nutrition: Calories 310 Fat 22.7 g Carbohydrates 16.1 g Protein 19.9 g

85. Green Bean Casserole

Preparation time: 15 minutes
Cooking time: 5 hours
Servings: 8
Ingredients:
- 2 (16 ounces) packages of frozen sliced green beans
- 2 tins of cream of chicken soup
- 2/3 cup of milk
- 1/2 cup grated Parmesan cheese
- 1/4 teaspoon of salt
- 1/4 teaspoon ground black pepper
- 1 (6 ounces) can of fried onions, divided

Directions:
1. Mix the green beans, cream of chicken soup, milk, Parmesan cheese, salt, black pepper, and half the can of fried onions in a slow cooker. Cover and cook on low for 5 to 6 hours. Top casserole with remaining French-fried onions to serve.

Nutrition: Calories 272 Fat 16.7 g Carbohydrates 22.9 g Protein 5.9 g

86. Texas Cowboy Baked Beans

Preparation time: 15 minutes
Cooking time: 2 hours

Servings: 12
Ingredients:
- 1-pound ground beef
- 4 cans of baked beans with pork
- 1 (4 ounces) can of canned chopped green chili peppers
- 1 small Vidalia onion, peeled and chopped
- 1 cup of barbecue sauce
- 1/2 cup of brown sugar
- 1 tablespoon garlic powder
- 1 tablespoon chili powder
- 3 tablespoons hot pepper sauce, to taste

Directions:
1. Fry the minced meat in a frying pan over medium heat until it is no longer pink; remove fat and set aside. In a 3 1/2 liter or larger slow cooker, combine the minced meat, baked beans, green chili, onion, and barbecue sauce.
2. Put the brown sugar, garlic powder, chili powder, plus hot pepper sauce. Bake for 2 hours on HIGH or low for 4 to 5 hours.

Nutrition: Calories 360 Fat 12.4 g Carbohydrates 50 g Protein 14.6 g

87. Frijoles La Charra

Preparation time: 15 minutes
Cooking time: 5 hours
Servings: 8

Ingredients:
- 1 pound of dry pinto beans
- 5 cloves of garlic, minced
- 1 teaspoon of salt
- 1/2 pound of bacon, diced
- 1 onion, minced
- 2 fresh tomatoes, diced
- 1 (3.5 ounces) can of sliced jalapeno peppers
- 1 can of beer
- 1/3 cup chopped fresh coriander

Directions:
1. Cook or brown the bacon in a frying pan over medium heat until it is evenly brown but still soft. Drain about half the fat. Put the onion in the frying pan, then cook until tender.
2. Mix in the tomatoes and jalapenos and cook until everything is hot. Transfer to the slow cooker and stir into the beans. Cover the slow cooker and continue cooking on low for 4 hours. Mix the beer and coriander about 30 minutes before the end of the cooking time.

Nutrition: Calories 353 Fat 13.8 g Carbohydrates 39.8 g Protein 16 g

88. Italian Flavored Salmon

Preparation Time: 15 minutes
Cooking Time: 2 hours 8 minutes
Servings: 6

Ingredients:
For Salmon:
- 1 tsp. Italian seasoning
- 1 tsp garlic powder
- ½ tsp red chili powder
- ½ tsp sweet paprika
- Salt
- ground black pepper
- 2 lb. skin-on salmon fillet
- Olive oil cooking spray
- 1 lemon, cut into slices
- 1 C. low-sodium vegetable broth
- 2 tbsp. fresh lemon juice

For Lemon Sauce:
- 2/3 C. heavy cream
- ¼ C. white wine
- 3 tbsp. fresh lemon juice
- 1/8 tsp. lemon zest, grated finely
- 2-3 tbsp. fresh parsley, chopped

Directions:
1. Line a slow cooker with a large piece of parchment paper. In a small bowl, mix the spices. Spray the salmon fillet with cooking spray and rub with cooking spray evenly.
2. In the center of the prepared slow cooker, arrange the lemon slices. Put the salmon fillet on top of lemon slices and pour the broth and lemon juice around the fish. Cook on low within 2 hours.
3. Prepare to preheat the oven to 400 degrees F. Uncover the slow cooker and transfer the salmon with liquid into a baking dish. Bake for about 5-8 minutes.
4. For the sauce, add the cream, wine, and lemon juice on medium-high heat and boil, frequently stirring in a small pan. Adjust the heat to low and simmer within 8 minutes. Uncover the pan and stir in the lemon zest.
5. Adjust the heat to high setting, then cook within 2 minutes. Remove from heat and set aside. Remove, then place the salmon fillet onto a cutting board. Cut the salmon into 4 equal-sized fillets and top with sauce. Garnish with parsley and serve.

Nutrition: Calories: 265 Carbohydrates: 1.8g Protein: 30.2g Fat: 14.6g Sugar: 0.4g Sodium: 115mg Fiber: 0.3g

89. Marvelous Salmon

Preparation Time: 15 minutes
Cooking Time: 2½ hours
Servings: 4

Ingredients:
- ¾ C. fresh cilantro leaves, chopped
- 2 garlic cloves, chopped finely
- 2-3 tbsp. fresh lime juice
- 1 tbsp. olive oil
- Salt, to taste
- 1 lb. salmon fillets

Directions:
1. Put all the ingredients except for salmon fillets and mix well in a medium bowl. In the bottom of a greased slow cooker, place the salmon fillets and top with garlic mixture. Cook on low within 2-2½ hours. With a spoon, mix the meat with pan juices and serve.

Nutrition: Calories: 184 Carbohydrates: 0.7g Protein: 22.2g Fat: 10.5g Sugar: 0.1g Sodium: 90mg Fiber: 0.1g

90. Nutrient-Packed Salmon

Preparation Time: 15 minutes
Cooking Time: 6 hours
Servings: 4

Ingredients:
- 1 tbsp. Italian seasoning
- 1 tsp. onion powder
- 1 tsp. garlic powder
- Salt
- ground black pepper
- 1 lb. salmon fillets
- 1 tbsp. olive oil
- 1 zucchini, quartered and sliced
- 1 red bell pepper, seeded and julienned
- 1 tomato, chopped
- ½ of onion, sliced
- 3 garlic cloves, sliced

Directions:
1. Generously, grease an oval as a Pyrex dish that will fit inside the slow cooker insert. Mix the Italian seasoning and spices in a small bowl. Season the salmon fillets with half of the spice mixture evenly and then coat with half of the oil.
2. In a large bowl, add the vegetables, remaining spice mixture, and oil and toss to coat well. Put the salmon fillets into the baking dish and top with

vegetables. With a piece of foil, cover the baking dish and place in the slow cooker. Cook on low within 6 hours. Serve hot.

Nutrition: Calories: 224 Carbohydrates: 7.9g Protein: 23.5g Fat: 11.8g Sugar: 4.1g Sodium: 98mg Fiber: 4.1g

91. Highly Nutritious Meal

Preparation Time: 20 minutes
Cooking Time: 5 hours 55 minutes
Servings: 6

Ingredients:
- ¾ C. French lentils
- ½ C. carrots, peeled and chopped finely
- ¼ C. celery, chopped finely
- ¼ C. red onion, chopped finely
- 1 bay leaf
- 2¼ C. low-sodium chicken broth
- 1 lb. small golden beets, scrubbed and trimmed
- 1 tbsp. olive oil
- Salt
- ground black pepper
- 1 tbsp. raw honey
- 3-4 tbsp. fresh orange juice
- 1 tbsp. orange zest, grated
- 2 tbsp. fresh lemon juice, divided
- 1 tsp. lemon zest, grated
- 6 (5-oz.) wild salmon fillets
- 2 tbsp. fresh parsley, chopped

Directions:
1. In a slow cooker, add the lentils, carrots, celery, onion, bay leaf, and broth and mix well. Arrange a piece of foil onto a smooth surface. In a bowl, add the beets, oil, salt, and black pepper and toss to coat well.
2. Place the beets in the center of foil and wrap tightly. Arrange the foil packet on top of the lentil mixture. Cook on low within 5-5½ hours. For the glaze, add the honey, juices, and zest over medium heat and boil in a small pan.
3. Adjust the heat to medium, then simmer for about 1-2 minutes, stirring continuously. Uncover the slow cooker and transfer the beets packet onto a plate. Unwrap the foil and set the beets aside to cool slightly. Peel the beets and cut into wedges.
4. Place 1 parchment paper over the lentil mixture in the slow cooker. Massage the salmon fillets with salt plus black pepper and brush the tops with glaze. Arrange the salmon fillets over the parchment, skin side down. Cook on low within 25 minutes.

5. Uncover the slow cooker and transfer the salmon fillets onto a platter. Discard the bay leaf and add the parsley, salt, and black pepper into lentil mixture. Serve lentils with salmon fillets and beet slices.

Nutrition: Calories: 407 Carbohydrates: 28g Protein: 38.4g Fat: 15.2g Sugar: 10.9g Sodium: 191mg Fiber: 9.5g

92. Super-Healthy Dinner

Preparation Time: 15 minutes
Cooking Time: 1 hour 15 minutes
Servings: 4

Ingredients:
- 2 lb. boneless cod fillets
- Salt, to taste
- 2 (14-oz.) cans diced tomatoes
- ½ C. Kalamata olives, pitted and sliced
- ¼ C. capers
- ½ of onion, sliced
- 6 garlic cloves, sliced
- 3 tbsp. fresh parsley, chopped roughly and divided
- 1 tsp. red pepper flakes, crushed
- Freshly ground black pepper, to taste
- 3 tbsp. olive oil, divided
- 1 lemon, sliced
- 1 C. couscous
- 1 C. hot boiling water

Directions:
1. Season each cod fillet with salt and set aside at room temperature for about 10-15 minutes. In a slow cooker, place the tomato, olives, capers, onion, garlic, 1 tbsp. of parsley, red pepper flakes, black pepper, and 1½ tbsp. olive oil and mix well.
2. Place the cod fillets over the sauce in a single layer and spoon some of the tomato mixtures on top. Arrange 2 lemon slices on top. Cook on high within 1 hour. Uncover the slow cooker and, with a slotted spoon, transfer the cod fillets onto a platter.
3. Place about 2/3 of the sauce on top of cod fillets. In your slow cooker with the remaining sauce, add the couscous, boiling water, and a little salt and mix well. Cook on high within 10 minutes. Uncover the slow cooker and with a fork fluff the couscous. Stir in the remaining olive oil and serve with cod fillets.

Nutrition: Calories: 507 Carbohydrates: 45.9g Protein: 48.7g Fat: 15.2g Sugar: 6g Sodium: 599mg Fiber: 6g

94. Paleo-Friendly Tilapia

Preparation Time: 15 minutes
Cooking Time: 2 hours
Servings: 4

Ingredients:
- 1 (15-oz.) can diced tomatoes
- 1 bell pepper, seeded and chopped
- 1 small onion, chopped
- 1 garlic clove, minced
- 1 tsp. dried rosemary
- 1/3 C. low-sodium chicken broth
- Salt
- ground black pepper
- 1 lb. tilapia fillets

Directions:
1. In a slow cooker, place all the ingredients except for tilapia and stir to combine. Place the tilapia on top and gently submerge in sauce. Cook on high within 2 hours. Serve hot.

Nutrition: Calories: 132 Carbohydrates: 8.5g Protein: 22.8g Fat: 1.4g Sugar: 5.1g Sodium: 92mg Fiber: 2.2g

95. Winner Halibut

Preparation Time: 10 minutes
Cooking Time: 2 hours
Servings: 2

Ingredients:
- 12 oz. halibut fillet
- Salt
- ground black pepper
- 1 tbsp. fresh lemon juice
- 1 tbsp. olive oil
- 1½ tsp. dried dill

Directions:
1. Arrange a large 18-inch piece of greased piece foil onto a smooth surface. Massage the halibut fillet with salt plus black pepper. In a small bowl, add the lemon juice, oil, and dill and mix well.
2. Put the halibut fillet in the center of foil and drizzle with oil mixture. Carefully bring up the edges of foil and crimp them, leaving plenty of air inside the foil packet.
3. Place the foil packet in the bottom of a slow cooker. Cook on high within 1½-2 hours. Uncover the slow cooker and remove the foil packet. Carefully open the foil packet and serve.

Nutrition: Calories: 258 Carbohydrates: 1.7g Protein: 36.4g Fat: 11.2g Sugar: 0.2g Sodium: 174mg Fiber: 0.4g

96. Unique Salmon Risotto

Preparation Time: 15 minutes
Cooking Time: 1 hour 20 minutes
Servings: 4

Ingredients:
- 2 tbsp. olive oil
- 2 shallots, chopped
- ½ of a medium cucumber, peeled, seeded, and chopped
- 1¼ C. Arborio rice
- 3 C. hot vegetable broth
- ½ C. white wine
- 1¼ lb. skinless salmon fillet, chopped
- Salt
- ground black pepper
- 1 scallion, chopped
- 3 tbsp. fresh dill, chopped

Directions:
1. In a pan, heat the oil over medium-high heat and sauté the shallot and cucumber for about 2-3 minutes. Cook on low within 15 minutes. Add the rice and stir to combine. Increase the heat to high and sauté for about 1 minute.
2. Remove from the heat and transfer the rice mixture into a slow cooker. Pour the hot broth and wine on top. Cook on high within 45 minutes, then stir in the salmon pieces, salt, and black pepper.
3. Cook on high within 15 minutes. Let the risotto stand, covered for about 5 minutes. Remove and stir in the scallion and dill. Serve hot.

Nutrition: Calories: 534 Carbohydrates: 53.2g Protein: 36.1g Fat: 17.3g Sugar: 1.5g Sodium: 686mg Fiber: 2.2g

97. Delish Dinner Shrimp

Preparation Time: 20 minutes
Cooking Time: 5 hours
Servings: 4

Ingredients:
- 1 medium onion, chopped
- ½ of medium green bell pepper, seeded and chopped
- 1 can whole tomatoes, undrained and chopped roughly
- 1 (2½-oz.) jar sliced mushrooms
- ¼ C. ripe olives, pitted and sliced
- 2 garlic cloves, minced
- 1 (14½-oz.) can low-sodium chicken broth
- 1 (8-oz.) can tomato sauce

- ½ C. dry white wine
- ½ C. orange juice
- 1 tsp. dried basil leaves
- 2 bay leaves
- ¼ tsp. fennel seed, crushed
- Salt
- ground black pepper
- 1 lb. medium shrimp, peeled

Directions:
1. In a slow cooker, place all the ingredients except for shrimp and mix. Cook on low within 4-4½ hours. Remove cover, then mix in the shrimp. Cook on low within 20-30 minutes. Uncover the slow cooker and discard the bay leaves. Serve hot.

Nutrition: Calories: 217 Carbohydrates: 16.9g Protein: 28.2g Fat: 2.8g Sugar: 10.2g Sodium: 705mg Fiber: 10.2g

98. Loveable Feta Shrimp

Preparation Time: 15 minutes
Cooking Time: 2 hours 25 minutes
Servings: 6

Ingredients:
- ¼ C. extra-virgin olive oil
- 1 medium onion, chopped
- 1 (28-oz.) can crushed tomatoes
- ½ C. dry white wine
- ½ tsp. dried oregano
- Pinch of red pepper flakes, crushed
- Salt, to taste
- 1½ lb. medium shrimp, peeled and deveined
- 1 C. feta cheese, crumbled
- 2 tbsp. fresh parsley, chopped

Directions:
1. Warm-up the oil over medium heat in a skillet and cook the onion for about 10 minutes, stirring frequently. Remove from the heat and transfer the onion into a large slow cooker. Add the tomatoes, wine, oregano, red pepper flakes, and salt and stir to combine.
2. Cook on high within 2 hours. Remove cover, then stir in the shrimp. Sprinkle with feta cheese evenly. Cook on high within 10-15 minutes. Serve hot with the garnishing of parsley.

Nutrition: Calories: 324 Carbohydrates: 14g Protein: 31.3g Fat: 15.1g Sugar: 9.4g Sodium: 819mg Fiber: 4.7g

99. Luncheon Party Meal

Preparation Time: 20 minutes

Cooking Time: 4½ hours
Servings: 4

Ingredients:
- 1 (14½-oz.) can diced tomatoes, drained
- 1 C. red sweet pepper, seeded and chopped
- 1 C. zucchini, sliced
- 2 garlic cloves, minced
- ½ C. dry white wine
- 8 oz. frozen medium shrimp, thawed
- 8 Kalamata olives, pitted and chopped roughly
- ¼ C. fresh basil, chopped
- 1 tbsp. olive oil
- 1½ tsp. fresh rosemary, chopped
- Salt, to taste
- 2 oz. feta cheese, crumbled

Directions:
1. In a greased slow cooker, put the tomatoes, sweet pepper, zucchini, garlic, and wine and mix well. Cook on low within 4 hours, then remove the cover and stir in the shrimp. Cook on high within 30 minutes. Uncover, then stir in the remaining ingredients. Serve hot with the topping of feta cheese.

Nutrition: Calories: 206 Carbohydrates: 10.8g Protein: 16.7g Fat: 8.9g Sugar: 5.5g Sodium: 423mg Fiber: 2.5g

100.   Easiest Shrimp Scampi

Preparation Time: 15 minutes
Cooking Time: 1½ hours
Servings: 4

Ingredients:
- 1 lb. raw shrimp, peeled and deveined
- ¼ C. chicken broth
- 2 tbsp. butter
- 2 tbsp. olive oil
- 1 tbsp. fresh lemon juice
- 1 tbsp. garlic, minced
- 1 tbsp. dried parsley
- Salt
- ground black pepper

Directions:
1. In a slow cooker, place all the ingredients and stir to combine. Cook on high within 1½ hours. Uncover the slow cooker and stir the mixture. Serve hot.

Nutrition: Calories: 252 Carbohydrates: 2.6g Protein: 26.4g Fat: 14.8g Sugar: 0.2g Sodium: 406mg Fiber: 0.1g

101. Amazingly Tasty Shrimp Orzo

Preparation Time: 15 minutes
Cooking Time: 3 hours 16 minutes
Servings: 6

Ingredients:
- 2 C. uncooked orzo pasta
- 2 tsp. dried basil
- 3 tbsp. olive oil, divided
- 2 tbsp. butter
- 1½ tbsp. shallot, chopped
- 1 (14½-oz.) can diced tomatoes, drained
- 3 garlic cloves, minced
- 2 tsp. dried oregano
- 1 lb. jumbo shrimp, peeled and deveined
- 1 C. oil-packed sun-dried tomatoes, chopped
- 1½ C. Greek olives pitted
- 2½ C. feta cheese, crumbled

Directions:
1. Cook the orzo within 8-10 minutes or according to the package's directions in a large pan of salted boiling water. Drain, then rinse under cold running water. Transfer the orzo into a large bowl with basil and 1 tbsp. of oil and toss to coat well. Set aside. Warm-up the remaining oil and butter over medium heat and sauté the shallot for about 2-3 minutes in a large skillet.
2. Put the tomatoes, garlic, plus oregano and cook within 1-2 minutes. Add the shrimp and sun-dried tomatoes and cook for about 1 minute. Remove from the heat and place the shrimp mixture into a greased slow cooker. Add the orzo mixture, olives, and cheese and stir. Cook on low within 2-3 hours. Serve hot.

Nutrition: Calories: 633 Carbohydrates: 57.9g Protein: 35.4g Fat: 30.2g Sugar: 8.5g Sodium: 1390mg Fiber: 5.3g

102. Delightful Shrimp Pasta

Preparation Time: 15 minutes
Cooking Time: 7¼ hours
Servings: 4

Ingredients:
- 1 (14½-oz.) can peeled tomatoes, chopped
- 1 (6-oz.) can tomato paste
- 2 tbsp. fresh parsley, minced
- 1 garlic clove, minced
- 1 tsp. dried oregano
- 1 tsp. dried basil
- 1 tsp. seasoned salt
- 1 lb. cooked shrimp
- Salt
- ground black pepper
- ¼ C. parmesan cheese, shredded

Directions:
1. In a slow cooker, place all the ingredients except for shrimp and Parmesan and stir to combine. Cook on low within 6-7 hours, then stir in the cooked shrimp. Sprinkle with parmesan cheese. Cook on high within 15 minutes. Serve hot.

Nutrition: Calories: 212 Carbohydrates: 14.6g Protein: 30.6g Fat: 3.8g Sugar: 7.9g Sodium: 828mg Fiber: 3.2g

103. Meltingly Tender Octopus

Preparation Time: 20 minutes
Cooking Time: 6 hours
Servings: 4

Ingredients:
- 1½ lb. octopus
- 6 fingerlings potatoes
- ½ lemon, cut into slices
- Salt
- ground black pepper
- Water, as required
- 3 tbsp. extra-virgin olive oil
- 3 tbsp. capers

Directions:
1. Remove the beak, eyes, and any other parts of the octopus, then rinse carefully. Slice off the head of the octopus at its base. In a pan of boiling water, dip the octopus with a pair of for about 10-15 seconds.
2. Now, place the octopus in a slow cooker. Place the potatoes, lemon slices, salt, black pepper, and enough water to cover. Cook on high within 5-6 hours. Uncover the slow cooker and drain the octopus in a colander.
3. With a slotted spoon, transfer the potatoes onto a platter. Pat dry the potatoes and slice it into thin. Cut the octopus into thin slices. In a large bowl, add the octopus, potatoes, oil, capers, salt, and black pepper and toss to coat. Serve immediately.

Nutrition: Calories: 308 Carbohydrates: 18.5g Protein: 30.6g Fat: 12.3g Sugar: 1.6g Sodium: 230mg Fiber: 3.3g

104.   Greek Shrimp and Feta Cheese

Preparation time: 15 minutes
Cooking time: 8 hours
Servings: 8

Ingredients:

- 2 Tablespoons extra virgin olive oil
- 1 medium onion, chopped
- 1 clove garlic, minced
- 1(28 oz.) canned San Marzano tomatoes
- 1(12 oz.) can tomato paste
- 1/4 cup dry white wine
- 2 tablespoons parsley, chopped
- 1 teaspoon dried oregano
- 1/4 teaspoon freshly ground black pepper
- 1 1/2-pound medium shrimp, peeled and deveined
- 2 oz. feta cheese, crumbled

Directions

1. In a medium sauté pan, heat olive oil until hot but not smoking. Add onion and cook about 4-5 minutes or until onions are soft. Add garlic and cook for 1 minute, do not brown. Mix all fixing except shrimp and feta in the slow cooker.
2. Cook on low within 6-8 hours. Adjust the heat to high; add shrimp, cook within 15 minutes, or until just pink. Stir in feta cheese and serve.

Nutrition: Calories 204 Fat: 7g Carbs: 15g Fiber: 3g Cholesterol: 136mg Protein: 21g Sodium: 689mg

105.   Basque Tuna with Potatoes and Peppers

Preparation time: 15 minutes
Cooking time: 4 hours
Servings: 6

Ingredients:

- 2 Tablespoons extra virgin olive oil
- 2 Tablespoons smoked paprika or more to taste
- 1 teaspoon kosher salt
- 1-1/2 lbs. fresh tuna, cut into 1-1/2-inch chunks
- 1 large sweet onion, cut into wedges
- 6 large cloves garlic, chopped
- 1 teaspoon freshly ground black pepper
- 1/2 cup dry white wine
- 2 cups San Marzano tomatoes, undrained
- 3 potatoes, unpeeled and cut into chunks
- 1 cup chicken stock
- 1 green bell pepper, cut into 3/4" pieces
- 1 red bell pepper, slice into 3/4" pieces
- 1/4 cup green olives, pitted
- 1/4 cup Kalamata olives, pitted
- 1 Tablespoon cornstarch
- Lemon wedges, for garnish

Directions:

1. In a bowl, combine olive oil, smoked paprika, salt, and tuna chunks. Toss until fish is well coated. Cover and refrigerate.
2. "Smoosh" the tomatoes up with your fingers and add to the slow cooker along with the onion, garlic, black pepper, wine, diced tomatoes, potatoes, and chicken stock. Cook on high within 2 hours or low within 4 hours.
3. Add the bell peppers and olives, and cook on high for 1 hour. Add the tuna chunks and the marinade. Cover and cook on high within 30 minutes. Transfer the tuna and vegetables to a serving bowl and cover to keep warm. Put the liquid from the crockpot into a small saucepan, and bring to a boil.
4. Place cornstarch in a small dish or measuring cup and add 2 tablespoons of cold water. Pour into the liquid in the saucepan in a small stream, stirring continuously. When it has thickened slightly, pour over the fish and vegetables. Garnish with lemon wedges. Serve hot, over polenta, couscous, or brown rice with a green salad and a crusty loaf of bread.

Nutrition: Calories: 317 Sodium: 630mg Carbs: 25.9g Fat: 11.9g Fiber: 4.8g Sugars: 5.5g Cholesterol: 23mg Protein: 23.2g

106.   Citrus Salmon

Preparation time: 15 minutes
Cooking time: 3 hours & 30 minutes
Servings: 6

Ingredients:

- 1 1/2 pounds salmon fillets
- Kosher salt
- Freshly ground white pepper to taste
- 1/4 cup freshly squeezed lemon juice
- 1teaspoon toasted sesame oil
- 2 teaspoons tamari
- A few drops of hot sauce
- 1 clove garlic, minced
- 1/2 cup scallions, sliced
- 5 Tablespoons fresh parsley, chopped
- 1 Tablespoon extra-virgin olive oil
- 2 teaspoons lemon zest
- 2 teaspoons orange zest
- Orange and lemon slices, for garnish
- Parsley, chopped, for garnish

Directions:

1. Butter slow cooker; and add lemon juice, sesame oil, tamari, hot sauce, and garlic to slow cooker. Sprinkle salmon fillets with salt and pepper. Place fish in a slow cooker.
2. Drizzle olive oil over salmon, top with scallions, parsley, orange, and lemon zest. Cook on low within 3 1/2 hours. Transfer salmon to serving platter and remove the skin. Serve garnished with orange and lemon slices and sprigs of fresh parsley.

Nutrition: Calories: 270 Sodium: 213mg Carbs: 1.6g Fat: 17.2g Fiber: 0.5g Sugars: 0.5g Cholesterol: 71mg Protein: 25.6g

107. Salmon with Mango Avocado Salsa

Preparation time: 15 minutes
Cooking time: 3 hours & 30 minutes
Servings: 6

Ingredients:

- 1 1/2 lbs. salmon fillets
- 1/4 cup cilantro stems removed, chopped
- 2 cloves garlic, minced
- 2-3 Tablespoons freshly squeezed lime juice
- 2 Tablespoons extra virgin olive oil
- 1/4 teaspoon kosher salt
- Freshly ground white pepper
- Mango Avocado Salsa

Directions:

1. Coat slow cooker with olive oil. Place fillets, skin side down, in the slow cooker. Top with cilantro. In a small bowl, combine garlic, lime juice, olive oil, salt, and white pepper.
2. Pour mixture over salmon. Cook on Low 3 1/2 hours. Transfer salmon to serving platter and remove the skin. Pour juices over the top and serve with Mango Avocado Salsa.

Nutrition: Calories: 275 Cholesterol: 71mg Sodium: 167mg Fat: 18.7g Carbs: 0.4g Protein: 25.1g

108. Salmon with Asparagus

Preparation time: 15 minutes
Cooking time: 3 hours & 30 minutes
Servings: 6

Ingredients:

- 1/2 cup water
- 1/2 cup chicken broth
- 1 cup dry white wine
- 1/2 thinly sliced small onion
- 3 sprigs tarragon, plus 1 tsp minced tarragon leaves
- 1/2 teaspoon kosher salt
- Freshly ground white pepper
- 1 1/2 lbs. salmon fillets
- 11/2 lbs. fresh asparagus spears, trimmed
- 1 Tablespoon butter
- 1 Tablespoon olive oil
- 1 large shallot, minced
- 2 teaspoons white wine vinegar

Directions:

1. Mix the water, broth, wine, onion, tarragon sprigs, salt, and white pepper in the slow cooker. Cook on low within 30 minutes.
2. Add the salmon fillets. Cover and cook on low within 3 hours or until salmon is opaque and tender. Transfer it to a serving platter, and remove the skin. Cover loosely to keep warm.
3. Discard the braising liquid and tarragon sprigs. During the last 30 minutes of salmon cooking time, over high heat, bring a large pot of lightly salted water to a boil.
4. Add asparagus spears and cook for about 4 minutes or until crisp-tender. Put into a colander in the sink and rinse well under cold running water, then pat dry.
5. Before you serve, heat butter and oil in a large skillet over medium heat until hot but not smoking. Add the shallot and cook for 2 or 3 minutes, or until slightly softened but not browned.
6. Add asparagus spears and stir to coat and warm thoroughly, then add the vinegar and minced tarragon, tossing to incorporate. Arrange asparagus spears around salmon fillets. Serve with parslied new red potatoes.

Nutrition: Calories: 392 Sodium: 351mg Carbs: 17.8g Fat: 18.9g Fiber: 8.9g Sugars: 8.4g Cholesterol: 77mg Protein: 34.7g

110.   Shrimp Marinara

Preparation time: 15 minutes
Cooking time: 8 hours
Servings: 8

Ingredients:
- 1 (28 oz.) can ground, peeled tomatoes
- 1 (12 oz.) can tomato paste
- 1/2 cup dry red wine
- 1/4 cup fresh parsley, minced
- 4 cloves garlic, minced
- 1 1/2 tsp. dried basil
- 2 teaspoon dried oregano
- 1 teaspoon kosher salt
- 1/4 teaspoon freshly ground black pepper
- 1/2 teaspoon seasoned salt
- 2 lb. medium shrimp, shelled, cooked, and thawed if frozen
- Grated Parmesan cheese, for garnish

Directions:
1. Combine tomatoes, tomato paste, red wine, parsley, garlic, basil, oregano, salt, pepper, and seasoned salt in a slow cooker.
2. Cover and cook on low within 7-8 hours. Adjust temperature to high, stir in cooked shrimp, cover and cook on high for about 15 minutes, or until just heated through. Serve over pasta, spaghetti squash, or polenta with a big green salad.

Nutrition: Calories: 243 Carbs: 18.4g Fiber: 4.6g Fat: 2.1g Sugars: 9.1g Cholesterol: 297mg Protein: 35.1g Sodium: 1294 mg

111.   Foil Wrapped Lemon Pepper Sole with Asparagus

Preparation time: 15 minutes
Cooking time: 4 hours
Servings: 4

Ingredients:
- 1 bunch asparagus, trimmed
- 1 1/2 lbs. sole filets, thawed if frozen
- 1/2 cup freshly squeezed lemon juice
- Lemon Pepper Seasoning
- 1/2 Tablespoon extra-virgin olive oil for each packet

Directions:
1. You will need a piece of foil for each serving large enough to wrap contents completely. Portion sole into 4 even portions, place each portion in the foil sheet center, and season with lemon pepper seasoning using approximately 1/4 teaspoon per

packet. Put 2 tablespoons of lemon juice and 1/2 tablespoon of olive oil.
2. Divide asparagus into 4 equal portions. Top sole with asparagus. Fold or flip the foil's sides over the sole and fold to close the foil up to form a packet. It should form a tightly wrapped packet.
3. Repeat this process with the remaining 3 portions. Place packets in the slow cooker, stacking if necessary. Cover and cook on high within 4 hours.

Nutrition: Calories: 213 Sodium: 125mg Carbs: 3.4g Fat: 9.0g Fiber: 1.7g Sugars: 1.8g Cholesterol: 77mg Protein: 29.2g

112.   Slow Cooker Chicken and Shrimp

Preparation time: 15 minutes
Cooking time: 8 hours & 20 minutes
Servings: 4

Ingredients:
- 1 lb. boneless, skinless chicken thighs
- 1/2 teaspoon kosher salt
- 1/8 teaspoon freshly ground black pepper
- 1/2 teaspoon crushed red pepper flakes
- 2 onions, chopped
- 6 cloves garlic, minced
- 1 (14 oz.) can season diced tomatoes, undrained
- 1 (8oz.) can tomato sauce
- 3 Tablespoons tomato paste
- 1 cup chicken broth
- 1 teaspoon dried thyme leaves
- 1/2 teaspoon dried basil leaves
- 3 Tablespoons lemon juice
- 1 (8 oz.) package frozen cooked shrimp, thawed
- 1 (12 oz.) can quarter artichoke hearts, drained
- 1 Tablespoon cornstarch
- 2/3 cup crumbled feta cheese

Directions:
1. Slice the chicken into large chunks, then season with salt and pepper to taste. Place onion and garlic in the bottom slow cooker and top with chicken.
2. Mix diced tomatoes, tomato sauce, tomato paste, chicken broth, thyme, basil, and lemon juice in a medium bowl. Pour over chicken. Cook on low within 6-8 hours until chicken is tender with the juices running clear or 165°F.on a thermometer.
3. Stir in thawed and drained shrimp and artichoke hearts. Put the cornstarch in a bowl, then add 2 tablespoons of water. Stir well to blend. Pour into a slow cooker.
4. Cover and cook within 15-20 minutes or until heated through and slightly thickened. Serve with

hot cooked pasta or couscous and sprinkle with feta cheese.

Nutrition: Calories: 369 Sodium: 701mg Carbs: 29.8g Fat: 11.1g Fiber: 7.8g Sugars: 17.4 Cholesterol: 162m Protein: 39.5g

113. Poached Swordfish with Lemon-Parsley Sauce

Preparation time: 15 minutes
Cooking time: 1 hour & 15 minutes
Servings: 4

Ingredients:
- 1 tablespoon butter
- 4 thin slices of sweet onion
- 2 cups of water
- 4 (6-ounce) swordfish steaks
- Kosher salt, to taste
- 1 lemon, thinly sliced, seeds removed
- 6 tablespoons extra-virgin olive oil
- 3 tablespoons fresh lemon juice
- 3/4 teaspoon Dijon mustard
- Freshly ground white pepper, to taste
- 3 tablespoons fresh flat-leaf parsley, minced
- 8 cups baby salad greens

Directions:
1. Butter the bottom and halfway up the side of the slow cooker. Arrange the onion slices on the slow cooker, then pour in the water. Cook on high within 30 minutes.
2. Salt and white pepper swordfish steaks to taste and place on onion slices. Top with lemon slices. Cover and cook on high within 45 minutes or until the fish is opaque. Remove from slow cooker and either wrap to keep warm or chill in the fridge.
3. In a bowl, combine oil, lemon juice, mustard, and white pepper, then mix the parsley. Split the sauce between the swordfish steaks. Toss 8 cups of salad greens with 2/3 of dressing. Arrange 2 cups of greens on each of 4 individual plates.
4. Place a hot or chilled swordfish steak on top of each plate of dressed greens. Spoon the remaining sauce over the fish.

Nutrition: Calories: 330 Sodium: 189mg Carbs: 3.2g Fat: 22.1g Fiber: 1.8g Sugars: 1.3g Protein: 29.9g

114. Easy Cheesy Salmon Loaf

Preparation time: 15 minutes
Cooking time: 3 hours & 20 minutes
Servings: 4

Ingredients:
- 1 tablespoon extra-virgin olive oil
- 1 (8 oz.) package sliced mushrooms
- 1 small onion, minced
- 1 can salmon, drained
- 1 1/2 cups fresh breadcrumbs
- 2 eggs, beaten
- 1 cup grated cheddar cheese
- 1 tablespoon lemon juice
- 1/4 teaspoon dry mustard
- 1 teaspoon Worcestershire sauce
- 1/2 teaspoon kosher salt
- 1 (10 oz.) package frozen peas, thawed, optional

Directions:
1. Cut three 24-in. x 3-inches strips of foil; crisscross. Put the strips on the bottom and up the sides of a slow cooker coated with cooking spray.
2. In a medium sauté pan, heat olive oil, add mushrooms and onion and sauté until vegetables are soft and liquid has evaporated.
3. Flake fish in the bowl, removing all bones. Add all remaining ingredients, including sautéed vegetables, excepting peas, and mix thoroughly.
4. Pour into a lightly greased crockpot or casserole dish and shape into a rounded loaf, pulling the foil strips up the side of the slow cooker so they can act as handles for removing salmon loaf.
5. Cover and cook on high within 1 hour, then reduce to low and cook for an additional 3 to 5 hours. If desired, top the salmon loaf with optional peas during the last hour of cooking.

Nutrition: Calories: 394 Sodium: 393mg Carbs: 22.3g Fat: 21.0g Fiber: 1.9g Sugars: 3.2g Cholesterol: 122mg Protein: 28.2g

115. Slow-Cooker Halibut Stew

Preparation time: 15 minutes
Cooking time: 9 hours
Servings: 6
Ingredients:
- 1 red bell pepper, slice into 3/4" pieces
- 1 small yellow onion, roughly chopped
- 2 carrots, thinly sliced
- 1 stalk celery, thinly sliced
- 1 large potato, peeled, cut into 1" pieces
- 1 1/2 cups clam broth or chicken stock
- 2 Tablespoons freshly squeezed lime juice
- 3 cloves garlic, minced
- 1/2 teaspoon freshly ground black pepper
- Kosher salt to taste
- 1 teaspoon chili powder
- 1/4 cup cilantro, chopped
- 1/2 teaspoon cumin
- 1/2 teaspoon red pepper flakes
- 1-pound halibut fillets, thawed if frozen, rinsed, and cut into bite-size pieces

- Cilantro, for garnish
- Lime wedges, for garnish

Directions:

1. Combine all the above ingredients in slow-cooker, except halibut and garnishes. Cover and cook on Low 8-9 hours. During the last 30 minutes, add halibut pieces, cover, and cook until halibut is opaque. Garnish with additional cilantro if desired.

Nutrition: Calories: 148 Sodium: 296 mg Fat: 2 g Carbs: 12 g Fiber: 2 g Sugars: 4 g Cholesterol: 26 mg Protein: 18 g

116.   Salmon and Green Beans

Preparation time: 15 minutes
Cooking time: 4 hours
Servings: 4

Ingredients:

- 1 1/4 lbs. salmon, thawed if frozen
- 1 lb. fresh green beans, washed and tops removed
- 1/4 cup tamari
- 1/4 cup honey
- 1 clove garlic, finely minced
- freshly ground white pepper, to taste
- 1 tablespoon fresh ginger, finely minced
- 1/4 cup freshly squeezed lemon juice
- 1/4 cup squeezed blood orange juice or substituted squeezed orange juice

Directions:

1. In a small bowl, combine tamari, honey, garlic, ginger, citrus juices, and white pepper. Wash and trim green beans, place in the slow cooker. Place fish on top of green beans.
2. Pour liquid mixture over the top. Cover and cook on low within 3-4 hours. Transfer salmon and green beans to a serving platter. Remove skin from salmon and drizzle juices over the top. Serve with quinoa or brown rice.

Nutrition: Calories: 279 Sodium: 736mg Carbs: 19.8g Fat: 11.9g Fiber: 2.9g Sugars: 14.0g Cholesterol: 60mg Protein: 23.8g

117.   Vegetable Ragout with Cornmeal Crusted Halibut Nuggets

Preparation time: 15 minutes
Cooking time: 10 hours
Servings: 6

Ingredients:

- 1 tablespoon extra-virgin olive oil
- 2 onions, finely chopped
- 2 carrots, peeled and finely chopped
- 1 teaspoon dried oregano
- 1 teaspoon kosher salt
- 1/2 teaspoon freshly ground black pepper
- 2 cups bottled clam juice or chicken stock
- 2 cups dry vermouth or dry white wine
- 2 cups, water
- 1 tablespoon freshly squeezed lime juice
- 2 potatoes cut into 1/2-inch dice
- 1 sweet potato, cut into 1" dice
- 1 red bell pepper, coarsely chopped
- 1/2 cup yellow cornmeal
- 1 teaspoon chili powder
- 1/4 teaspoon cayenne pepper
- kosher salt
- ground black pepper
- 1 1/2 pounds, halibut, cut into 1/2-inch pieces
- 2 tablespoons extra virgin olive oil for frying halibut
- sour cream, garnish
- lime wedges, garnish

Directions:

1. In a large sauté pan, heat the 1 Tablespoon of oil over medium heat until hot but not smoking. Add chopped onions, carrots, and celery. Cook, stirring until the carrots are softened, about 7 minutes.
2. Add oregano, salt, and pepper and cook, stirring, for 1 minute. Transfer to a slow cooker. Add clam juice or broth, vermouth, water, and lime juice. Add the potatoes and sweet potatoes and stir to combine. Cover and cook on low for 8-10 hours or on high for 4-5 hours or until vegetables are tender.
3. Stir in the bell pepper. Cover the pot once again and cook on high for 20 minutes or until the bell pepper is soft. In a zip-top plastic bag, mix the cornmeal and chili powder. Add the halibut pieces and toss gently until the pieces are evenly coated.
4. In a medium sauté pan, heat the remaining 2 tablespoons olive oil over medium-high heat until hot but not smoking. Add halibut pieces, in batches if necessary, and sauté, turning once, until the fish pieces are nicely browned.
5. Discard any excess cornmeal mixture. Put the stew into serving bowls and top with browned halibut nuggets. Top with a dollop of sour cream, add a lime wedge, and serve.

Nutrition: Calories: 430 Sodium: 506mg Carbs: 33.9g Fat: 11.1g Fiber: 5.5g Sugars: 7.3g Cholesterol: 46mg Protein: 35.0g

118.   Salmon with Lemon and Green Olive Sauce

Preparation time: 15 minutes
Cooking time: 6 hours
Servings: 6

Ingredients:

- Extra virgin olive oil for coating slow cooker
- 1 large lemon, thinly sliced and seeds removed
- 2 medium shallots, thinly sliced
- 1/2 cup water
- 1 1/2 pounds thick salmon fillet, cut into 6 pieces
- 2 Tablespoons extra virgin olive oil
- Kosher salt and freshly ground black pepper

Sauce:

- 2 tablespoons extra virgin olive oil
- 1 tablespoon freshly squeezed lemon juice
- 1/2 teaspoon lemon zest
- 1/2 teaspoon dried oregano
- kosher salt and freshly ground black pepper
- 1/2 cup pitted green olives, chopped
- 1 tablespoon fresh flat-leaf parsley, chopped
- 1 tablespoon capers, rinsed

Directions:

1. Grease your slow cooker with extra virgin olive oil. Drop half of the shallots into the bottom of the slow cooker. Add half the lemon slices and water.
2. Massage the salmon with olive oil and sprinkle with salt and pepper, to taste. Place salmon skin-side down in the slow cooker. Top with remaining lemon slices and shallot.
3. Cover and cook on low for 60-75 minutes, or until the salmon is opaque and cooked through. While salmon is cooking, make the sauce:
4. Mix the olive oil, lemon juice, zest, oregano, salt, and pepper to taste in a small bowl. Stir in olives, parsley, and capers. Transfer salmon to individual plates, remove the skin and drizzle with sauce.
5. It's also excellently served at room temperature on a bed of baby greens accompanied by a loaf of crusty bread.

Nutrition: Calories: 318 Cholesterol: 71mg Sodium: 113mg Fat: 23.4g Carbs: 0.8g Protein: 25.2g

119.   Salmon with Dill and Shallots

Preparation time: 15 minutes
Cooking time: 6 hours
Servings: 6

Ingredients:

- 4 large shallots, thinly sliced
- 1/4 cup dry white wine
- 1 cup of water
- 1 1/2 lbs. boneless salmon fillet
- 1 Tablespoon extra-virgin olive oil
- Kosher salt
- ground black pepper
- 2 Tablespoons freshly squeezed lemon juice
- 3 or 4 sprigs fresh dill, chopped or 1/2 tsp. dried dill weed
- 1 lemon, sliced and seeds removed

Directions:

1. Rinse salmon on both sides and pat dry with paper towels. With skin side down, cut into 6 even portions. Sprinkle shallots in the bottom of the slow cooker. Pour wine and water over. Mix oil and dill and spoon over the top of salmon.
2. Rub oil in to make sure salmon is evenly coated with oil. Place salmon pieces in the slow cooker, skin side down. Put the lemon juice and season with salt and pepper.
3. Top with lemon slices and cover, and cook on low for 90 minutes. Gently remove salmon from slow cooker with a slotted spatula. Remove skin. Serve warm with thyme roasted sweet potatoes and a green salad.

Nutrition: Calories: 341 Cholesterol: 95mg Sodium: 95mg Fat: 21.0 Carbs: 0.4g Protein: 33.5g

121. Calamari Stuffed with Sausage and Raisins

Preparation time: 15 minutes
Cooking time: 2 hours
Servings: 6

Ingredients:

- 1 1/2 pounds large squid (about 10 to 12)
- 3 tablespoons olive oil, divided
- 1/4-pound bulk sweet Italian sausage
- 2 shallots, minced
- 2 garlic cloves, minced
- 1/2 cup cooked white rice
- 2 tablespoons finely chopped raisins
- Salt
- ground black pepper
- 1 cup Herbed Tomato Sauce or purchased marinara sauce
- 1/3 cup dry white wine
- Toothpicks

Directions:

1. Rinse squid inside and out, and clean if necessary. Chop the tentacles very finely, and set aside. Warm a 1 tablespoon oil in a medium skillet over medium-high heat.
2. Crumble sausage into the skillet, and cook, breaking up lumps with a fork, for 2 minutes. Put the shallots and garlic, and cook within 3 minutes, or until shallots begin to soften.
3. Put the batter into a mixing bowl, add rice, raisins, and squid tentacles, put salt and pepper and stir well. Stuff a portion of stuffing into each squid, and close each tightly with toothpicks. Warm-up the rest of the oil in the skillet over medium-high heat.
4. Add squid, and brown on both sides, turning them gently with tongs. Transfer squid to the slow cooker, and add tomato sauce and wine.
5. Cook on high within 1 hour, then reduce the heat to low, and cook for 1 to 1 1/2 hours or until the squid are tender when pierced with the tip of a parking knife. Remove squid from the slow cooker with a slotted spoon, and discard toothpicks. Season sauce to taste with salt and pepper, and serve hot.

Nutrition: Calories: 223 Carbs: 11g Fat: 11g Protein: 19g

122. Calamari with Garbanzo Beans and Greens

Preparation time: 15 minutes
Cooking time: 1 hour & 30 minutes
Servings: 6

Ingredients:

- 1 large bunch of Swiss chard
- 1 1/2 pounds cleaned squid
- 1/4 cup olive oil
- 1 medium onion, diced
- 2 garlic cloves, minced
- 1 carrot, chopped
- 1 (14.5-ounce) can diced tomatoes, undrained
- 1/2 cup Seafood Stock or purchased stock
- 1/2 cup dry white wine
- 2 tablespoons chopped fresh parsley
- 1 tbsp. chopped oregano
- 1/2-1 tsp crushed red pepper flake
- 1 can garbanzo beans, drained
- Salt
- ground black pepper to taste

Directions:

1. Boil a pot of salted water, and have a bowl of ice water handy. Discard tough stems from Swiss chard, and cut leaves into 1-inch slices. Boil Swiss chard for 2 minutes, then drain and plunge into ice water to stop the cooking action. Drain again, and transfer Swiss chard to the slow cooker.
2. Rinse squid inside and out, and clean if necessary. Cut bodies into rings 3/4-inch wide, and leave tentacles whole. Set aside. Warm-up oil in a medium skillet over medium-high heat. Add onion, garlic, carrot, and cook, frequently stirring, for 5 minutes, or until onions soften.
3. Add tomatoes, stock, wine, parsley, oregano, and red pepper flakes to the skillet, and bring to a boil over high heat. Pour mixture into the slow cooker. Add squid to the slow cooker, and stir well. Cook on low for 2 to 4 hours, or on high for 1 to 2 hours, or until squid is tender. If cooking on low, raise the heat to high.
4. Put the garbanzo beans, and cook within 15 minutes, or until heated through. Sea- son to taste with salt and pepper, and serve hot.

Nutrition: Calories: 216 Carbs: 34g Fat: 4g Protein: 0g

124.   Tomato-Braised Tuna

Preparation time: 15 minutes
Cooking time: 1 hour & 30 minutes
Servings: 4

Ingredients:

- 1 (1^1/2 to 2 pound) tuna fillet in one thick slice
- ^{1}/4 cup olive oil, divided
- ^{1}/2 small red onion, chopped
- 3 garlic cloves, minced
- 1^1/2 cups Herbed Tomato Sauce or purchased marinara sauce
- ^{1}/2 cup dry white wine
- 3 tablespoons capers, drained and rinsed
- 2 tablespoons chopped fresh parsley
- 1 bay leaf
- Salt
- ground black pepper

Directions:

1. Soak tuna in cold salted water for 10 minutes. Pat dry with paper towels. 2. Heat 2 tablespoons oil in a large skillet over medium-high heat. Put the onion plus garlic, and cook, frequently stirring, for 3 minutes.
2. Scrape mixture into the slow cooker. Add tomato sauce, wine, capers, parsley, and bay leaf to the slow cooker, and stir well. Cook on high for 1 hour.
3. Warm-up the rest of the oil in the skillet over medium-high heat. Add tuna and brown well on both sides. Add tuna to the slow cooker, and cook on high for an additional 1 to 1^1/2 hours or until tuna is cooked but still rare in the center. Remove the bay leaf, season to taste with salt and pepper, and serve hot.

Nutrition: Calories: 101 Carbs: 3g Fat: 1g Protein: 19g

125.   Fish with Tomatoes and Fennel

Preparation time: 15 minutes
Cooking time: 3 hours
Servings: 6

Ingredients:

- 2 medium fennel bulbs
- ^{1}/4 cup olive oil
- 1 large onion, thinly sliced
- 2 garlic cloves, minced
- 1 (28-ounce) can diced tomatoes, drained
- ^{1}/2 cup dry white wine
- 1 tablespoon grated orange zest
- ^{1}/2 cup freshly squeezed orange juice
- 1 tablespoon fennel seeds, crushed
- 2 pounds thick firm-fleshed white fish fillets, cut into serving-sized pieces
- Salt
- ground black pepper

Directions:

1. Discard stalks from fennel, and save for another use. Rinse fennel, cut in half lengthwise, and discard core and the top layer of flesh. Slice fennel thinly and set aside.
2. Warm-up oil in a large skillet on medium-high heat. Put the onion and garlic, and cook, for 3 minutes, or until onion is translucent. Add fennel and cook for an additional 2 minutes. Scrape mixture into the slow cooker.
3. Add tomatoes, wine, orange zest, orange juice, and fennel seeds to the slow cooker, and stir well. Cook on low within 5 to 7 hours or on high for 2^1/2 to 3 hours, or until fennel is crisp-tender.
4. If cooking on low, raise the heat to high. Massage the fish with salt plus pepper, and place it on top of vegetables. Cook within 30 to 45 minutes. Put salt and pepper, and serve hot.

Nutrition: Calories: 317 Carbs: 0g Fat: 8g Protein: 40g

127.   Monkfish with Cabbage, Pancetta, and Rosemary

Preparation time: 15 minutes
Cooking time: 2 hours
Servings: 6

Ingredients:
- $^1/2$ small ($1^1/2$-pound) head Savoy or green cabbage
- $^1/4$-pound pancetta, diced
- 2 pounds monkfish fillets, trimmed and cut into serving pieces
- 2 garlic cloves, minced
- 1 cup Seafood Stock or purchased stock
- 2 tbsp. chopped fresh rosemary
- 1 tablespoon chopped fresh parsley
- 2 teaspoons grated lemon zest
- Salt
- ground black pepper to taste
- 2 tablespoons unsalted butter

Directions:
1. Rinse and core cabbage. Cut into wedges and then shred the cabbage. Boil a large pot of salted water. Add cabbage and boil for 4 minutes. Drain the cabbage and place it in the slow cooker.
2. Cook pancetta in a heavy skillet over medium heat for 5 to 7 minutes, or until crisp. Remove pancetta, and place it in the slow cooker. Raise the heat to high, and sear monkfish in the fat on all sides, turning the pieces gently with tongs, until browned. Refrigerate monkfish.
3. Add garlic, stock, rosemary, parsley, and lemon zest to the slow cooker, and stir well. Cook on low within 3 to 4 hours or on high for $1^1/2$ to 2 hours, or until cabbage is almost tender.
4. If cooking on low, raise the heat to high. Season monkfish with salt and pepper, and place it on top of vegetables. Cook monkfish for 30 to 45 minutes, or until it is cooked through.
5. Remove monkfish from the slow cooker, and keep it warm. Add butter to cabbage, and stir to melt butter. Season to taste with salt and pepper. To serve, mound equal size portions of cabbage on each plate. Slice monkfish into medallions, and arrange on top of the cabbage.

Nutrition: Calories: 84 Carbs: 2g Fat: 2g Protein: 14g

128.   Poached Fish with Vegetables and Herbs

Preparation time: 15 minutes
Cooking time: 2 hours
Servings: 6

Ingredients:
- 1-pound thick firm-fleshed white fish fillets, cut into serving pieces
- $^1/4$ cup olive oil, divided
- Salt
- ground black pepper
- 1 large sweet onion, thinly sliced
- 2 celery ribs, sliced
- $^1/2$ small fennel bulb, trimmed, cored, and thinly sliced
- 2 cups Seafood Stock or purchased stock
- 1 (14.5-ounce) can diced tomatoes, undrained
- $^1/2$ cup dry white wine
- $^1/2$ cup chopped fresh parsley, divided
- 2 tbsp. chopped fresh oregano
- 2 teaspoons grated lemon zest
- 1 bay leaf
- $^1/2$-pound large shrimp, peeled and deveined
- 1 dozen littleneck clams, well-scrubbed

Directions:
1. Drizzle the fish with two tablespoons of olive oil, then put salt and pepper. Refrigerate, tightly covered with plastic wrap. Warm-up oil in a large skillet over medium-high heat. Add onion, celery, and fennel, and cook, frequently stirring, for 3 minutes, or until onion is translucent. Scrape mixture into the slow cooker.
2. Add stock, tomatoes, wine, 3 tablespoons parsley, oregano, lemon zest, and bay leaf to the slow cooker, and stir well. Cook on low within 4 to 5 hours or on high for 2 to $2^1/2$ hours, or until vegetables are crisp-tender.
3. If cooking on low, raise the heat to high. Add fish, shrimp, and clams, and cook for 45 minutes to 1 hour. Remove the bay leaf, and put salt plus pepper. Serve hot, sprinkling each serving with remaining parsley.

Nutrition: Calories: 223 Carbs: 2g Fat: 5g Protein: 37g

129. Poached Chicken Breasts

Preparation time: 15 minutes
Cooking time: 8 hours
Servings: 6

Ingredients:
- 1 leek, sliced
- 1 shallot, diced
- 2 cloves garlic, minced
- 1 large carrot, peeled and diced
- 1 stalk celery, diced
- 11/2 pounds boneless, skinless chicken breasts
- 1/4 cup dry white wine
- 1 cup Roasted Chicken Broth
- 1/4 cup olive oil

Directions:
1. Grease a 4- to 5-quart slow cooker using a nonstick olive oil cooking spray. Place all of the fixings in the cooker. Cover and cook on low within 7–8 hours. Serve each breast with some of the cooking liquid and a drizzle of olive oil.

Nutrition: Calories: 252 Fat: 13g Protein: 25g Sodium: 322mg Fiber: 1g Carbohydrates: 7g Sugar: 2g

130. Rosemary Chicken with Potatoes

Preparation time: 15 minutes
Cooking time: 4 hours & 10 minutes
Servings: 6

Ingredients:
- 1 tablespoon olive oil
- 2 pounds boneless, skinless chicken thighs
- 1/2 teaspoon kosher salt
- 1/2 teaspoon freshly ground black pepper
- 6 small red potatoes, halved
- 1 leek (white and pale green parts only), sliced into 1" pieces
- 6 sprigs rosemary, divided
- 1 garlic clove, minced
- 1/2 cup Roasted Chicken Broth
- 1/4 cup capers

Directions:
1. Warm-up the olive oil in a large skillet over medium heat until hot but not smoking. Put the chicken and massage with salt and pepper. Cook within 5 minutes on one side and flip. Cook for an additional 5 minutes.

2. Place the potatoes and leek into a 4- to 5-quart slow cooker. Top with 5 sprigs of rosemary and garlic. Place chicken thighs on the rosemary. Pour broth over chicken and potatoes. Cover and cook on high within 3–4 hours. Put capers before serving, and garnish with remaining rosemary.

Nutrition: Calories: 336 Fat: 9g Protein: 33g Sodium: 595mg Fiber: 3g Carbohydrates: 30g Sugar: 2g

131. Sage Ricotta Chicken Breasts

Preparation time: 15 minutes
Cooking time: 8 hours & 6 minutes
Servings: 4

Ingredients:
- 6 fresh sage leaves, chopped
- 1/2 cup part-skim ricotta cheese
- 4 (4-ounce) boneless, skinless chicken breasts
- 1/2 teaspoon kosher salt
- 1/2 teaspoon freshly ground black pepper
- 1 tablespoon olive oil
- 1/2 cup white wine
- 3/4 cup chicken broth
- 1/4 cup niçoise olives, pitted and chopped

Directions:
1. Combine sage and ricotta in a small bowl. Gently slice a slit into a chicken breast to form a pocket. Stuff 2 tablespoons of filling into the chicken. Tie with kitchen twine and trim ends. Repeat with the rest of the chicken and cheese.
2. Flavor the chicken breasts with salt plus pepper. Heat olive oil in a large skillet until it's hot but not smoking. Place chicken in the skillet and sear on one side, about 3 minutes. Flip and brown on the second side, about 3 minutes.
3. Gently place chicken in a 4- to 5-quart slow cooker. Pour wine and chicken broth into the slow cooker. Cook on low for 6–8 hours. Cut twine from chicken breasts and sprinkle with olives.

Nutrition: Calories: 168 Fat: 7g Protein: 19g Sodium: 489mg Fiber: 0g Carbohydrates: 3g Sugar: 0g

133.   Sweet and Tangy Duck

Preparation time: 15 minutes
Cooking time: 4 hours & 4 minutes
Servings: 6

Ingredients:
- 1 (3-pound) duckling, skin removed
- 1 tablespoon olive oil
- 1/2 teaspoon kosher salt
- 1/2 teaspoon freshly ground black pepper
- 1/2 teaspoon red pepper flakes
- 2 cloves garlic, minced
- 1 medium apple, cut into 1" pieces
- 1 medium pear, peeled, slice into 1" pieces
- 1 tablespoon lemon juice
- 1 large red onion, peeled and chopped
- 1 large carrot, peeled and chopped
- 1 stalk celery, chopped
- 1/2 cup dry red wine
- 1/4 cup honey
- 1/4 cup cider vinegar
- 1 cup Roasted Chicken Broth

Directions:
1. Remove any extraneous fat from the duck. Cut into serving-size portions. Warm-up the olive oil in a large skillet or Dutch oven until hot but not smoking. Add the duck and season with salt, pepper, and red pepper flakes.
2. Cook for 3 minutes on one side. Add garlic to the pan, flip the duck, and cook for 1 minute. While the duck is browning, place apple and pear pieces in a bowl of cold water with lemon juice.
3. Put the onion, carrot, and celery in the bottom of a 4- to 5-quart slow cooker. Drain the apple and pear, and top vegetables with the duck and apple and pear mixture.
4. In a small bowl, whisk the wine, honey, vinegar, and broth. Pour over the duck. Cover and cook on high within 3–4 hours.

Nutrition: Calories: 422 Fat: 12g Protein: 46 Sodium: 516mg Fiber: 2g Carbohydrates: 26g Sugar: 19g

134.   Classic Chicken Parmesan

Preparation time: 15 minutes
Cooking time: 4 hours & 13 minutes
Servings: 4

Ingredients:
- 1 large egg
- 1/2 cup bread crumbs
- 1/2 teaspoon dried basil
- 1/2 teaspoon dried oregano
- 6 (4-ounce) boneless, skinless chicken breast halves
- 1 tablespoon olive oil
- 13/4 cups Tomato Sauce
- 1/2 cup shredded mozzarella cheese
- 2 tablespoons grated Parmesan cheese
- 1/4 cup chopped fresh parsley

Directions:
1. Mix the egg until foamy in a shallow dish. Mix the bread crumbs, basil, and oregano in another shallow dish. Soak the chicken in the egg, then into the bread crumb mixture to coat.
2. Warm-up olive oil in a large skillet until hot but not smoking. Put the chicken and brown within 3 minutes. Flip, and cook again within 3 minutes.
3. Put the chicken in a 4- to 5-quart slow cooker. Cover with tomato sauce. Cook on high for 3–4 hours. Sprinkle with cheeses, turn heat to low, and cook for 10 minutes. Remove from slow cooker and garnish with parsley.

Nutrition: Calories: 278 Fat: 11g Protein: 32g Sodium: 732mg Fiber: 1.5g Carbohydrates: 11g Sugar: 4g

135.   Lemony Roast Chicken

Preparation time: 15 minutes
Cooking time: 7 hours
Servings: 6

Ingredients:
- 1 (31/2- to 4-pound) frying chicken
- 1 teaspoon kosher salt
- 1 teaspoon freshly ground black pepper
- 1 clove garlic, crushed
- 3 tablespoons olive oil
- 2 lemons, quartered
- 1/2 cup Roasted Chicken Broth

Directions:
1. Massage the chicken with salt, pepper, plus garlic. Brush with olive oil. Put the lemon quarters in the slow cooker. Top with the chicken. Pour the broth over the chicken. Cover and cook on high within 1 hour. Adjust the heat to low and cook for 5–6 hours.

Nutrition: Calories: 608 Fat: 20g Protein: 96g Sodium: 825mg Fiber: 1g Carbohydrates: 3g Sugar: 0.5g

137. Cornish Game Hens

Preparation time: 15 minutes
Cooking time: 5 hours & 10 minutes
Servings: 2

Ingredients:

- 2 (11/2-pound) game hens
- 1 teaspoon kosher salt, divided
- 1 teaspoon freshly ground black pepper, divided
- 2 scallions, finely diced
- 2 fresh mint leaves, chopped
- 1/4 cup coarse cornmeal
- 2 tablespoons olive oil, divided
- 1/2 cup White Wine Vegetable Stock

Directions:

1. Wash the hens inside and out. Pat dry. Season the inside of each with half of the salt and pepper. Combine scallions, mint, and cornmeal in a small bowl. Place 2 tablespoons of the cornmeal mixture in the cavity of each hen. Pull loose skin over the cavity and secure with kitchen string.
2. Warm-up 1 tablespoon of olive oil in a large skillet over medium heat until hot but not smoking. Massage the hens with the rest of the salt and pepper. Place hens in the pan and cook for 5 minutes. Flip and brown for 5 minutes more.
3. Grease inside of a 4-5-quart slow cooker with 2 teaspoons olive oil. Use the rest of the olive oil to brush on the hens. Place hens in the slow cooker and pour in the stock. Cover and cook on high within 4–5 hours. The stuffing temperature should read 165 F with an instant-read thermometer.

Nutrition: Calories: 991 Fat: 34g Protein: 145g Sodium: 1,837mg Fiber: 1g Carbohydrates: 16g Sugar: 1g

138. Mediterranean Chicken Casserole

Preparation time: 15 minutes
Cooking time: 6 hours
Servings: 4

Ingredients:

- 1 medium butternut squash, 2" cubes
- 1 medium bell pepper, seeded and diced
- 1 (141/2-ounce) can diced tomatoes, undrained
- 4 boneless, skinless chicken breast halves, bite-sized pieces
- 1/2 cup mild salsa
- 1/4 cup raisins
- 1/4 teaspoon ground cinnamon
- 1/4 teaspoon ground cumin
- 2 cups cooked white rice
- 1/4 cup chopped fresh parsley

Directions:

1. Add squash and bell pepper to the bottom of a greased 4- to 5-quart slow cooker. Mix tomatoes, chicken, salsa, raisins, cinnamon, and cumin and pour on top of squash and peppers.
2. Cover and cook on low within 6 hours or on high for 3 hours. Remove chicken and vegetables, then serve over cooked rice. Spoon remaining sauce from slow cooker over the vegetables. Garnish with parsley.

Nutrition: Calories: 317 Fat: 3g Protein: 28.5g Sodium: 474mg Fiber: 3g Carbohydrates: 43g Sugar: 10g

139. Chicken Pesto Polenta

Preparation time: 15 minutes
Cooking time: 6 hours & 45 minutes
Servings: 6

Ingredients:

- 4 boneless, skinless chicken breasts, bite-sized pieces
- 1 cup prepared pesto, divided
- 1 medium onion, peeled and finely diced
- 4 cloves garlic, minced
- 11/2 teaspoons dried Italian seasoning
- 1 (16-ounce) tube prepared polenta, cut into 1/2" slices
- 2 cups chopped fresh spinach
- 1 (141/2-ounce) can diced tomatoes
- 1 (8-ounce) bag shredded low-fat Italian cheese blend

Directions:

1. Mix the chicken pieces with pesto, onion, garlic, and Italian seasoning in a large bowl. Layer half of the chicken mixture, half the polenta, half the spinach, and half the tomatoes in a greased 4- to 5-quart slow cooker.
2. Continue to layer, ending with tomatoes. Cover and cook on low within 4–6 hours or on high for 2–3 hours. Top with cheese. Cover and continue to cook for 45 minutes to an hour until cheese has melted.

Nutrition: Calories: 535 Fat: 16g Protein: 32g Sodium: 429mg Fiber: 4g Carbohydrates: 65g Sugar: 4g

140.   Rotisserie-Style Chicken

Preparation time: 15 minutes
Cooking time: 5 hours & 15 minutes
Servings: 6

Ingredients:
- 1 (4-pound) whole chicken
- 11/2 teaspoons kosher salt
- 2 teaspoons paprika
- 1/2 teaspoon onion powder
- 1/2 teaspoon dried thyme
- 1/2 teaspoon dried basil
- 1/2 teaspoon ground white pepper
- 1/2 teaspoon ground cayenne pepper
- 1/2 teaspoon ground black pepper
- 1/2 teaspoon garlic powder
- 2 tablespoons olive oil

Directions:
1. In a small bowl, mix salt, paprika, onion powder, thyme, basil, white pepper, cayenne pepper, black pepper, plus garlic powder. Massage with the spice mixture the entire chicken.
2. Place the spice-rubbed chicken in a greased 6-quart slow cooker. Drizzle olive oil evenly over the chicken. Cook on high for 3–31/2 hours or on low for 4–5 hours. Remove chicken carefully from the slow cooker and place on a large plate or serving platter.

Nutrition: Calories: 400 Fat: 14g Protein: 64g Sodium: 820mg Fiber: 0.5g Carbohydrates: 1g Sugar: 0g

141.   Spicy Olive Chicken

Preparation time: 15 minutes
Cooking time: 6 hours
Servings: 4

Ingredients:
- 1 whole chicken, slice into 8 pieces
- 1 teaspoon kosher salt
- 1/2 teaspoon ground black pepper
- 4 tablespoons unsalted butter
- 2/3 cup chopped sweet onion
- 2 tablespoons capers, drained and rinsed
- 24 green olives, pitted
- 1/2 cup chicken broth
- 1/2 cup dry white wine
- 1 teaspoon prepared Dijon mustard
- 1/2 teaspoon hot sauce
- 2 cups cooked white rice
- 1/4 cup fresh chopped parsley

Directions:

1. Massage the chicken pieces with salt plus pepper and then brown them in the butter in a large skillet over medium-high heat within 3 minutes on each side. Remove chicken from skillet and place in a greased 4- to 5-quart slow cooker.
2. Sauté the onion in the same skillet for an additional 3–5 minutes. Add onion to slow cooker, along with capers and olives.
3. In a small bowl, whisk the broth, wine, and mustard. Pour over chicken in the slow cooker. Add hot sauce. Cover and cook on high within 3–31/2 hours or low for 51/2–6 hours. When ready to serve, place the chicken over rice. Spoon sauce and olives over each serving. Garnish with parsley.

Nutrition: Calories: 703 Fat: 25g Protein: 75g Sodium: 1,373mg Fiber: 2g Carbohydrates: 34g Sugar: 1.5g

142.   Sun-Dried Tomato and Feta Stuffed Chicken

Preparation time: 15 minutes
Cooking time: 6 hours
Servings: 4

Ingredients:
- 4 (4-ounce) boneless, skinless chicken breasts
- 1/2 cup chopped oil-packed sun-dried tomatoes
- 1/3 cup crumbled feta cheese
- 1/4 cup chopped pitted Kalamata olives
- 11/2 cups fresh baby spinach leaves
- 2 tablespoons olive oil
- 1/2 teaspoon kosher salt
- 1/2 teaspoon freshly ground black pepper

Directions:
1. Flatten chicken breasts on a wooden cutting board with a meat mallet's flat side, to 1/2-inch thick. Set chicken breasts aside.
2. In a small bowl, mix the tomatoes, cheese, and olives. Place 3–4 spinach leaves in the middle of each flattened chicken breast. Place 2–3 tablespoons of the tomato filling on top of the spinach leaves.
3. Fold one side of the flattened chicken breast over the filling and continue to roll into a cylinder; secure with 2–3 toothpicks per chicken breast. Place the chicken rolls seam-side down in a greased 4- to 5-quart slow cooker.
4. Drizzle olive oil evenly over the top of the chicken rolls and sprinkle the chicken with salt and pepper. Cook on high within 3 hours or on low for 6 hours.

Nutrition: Calories: 248 Fat: 12.5g Protein: 27g Sodium: 715mg Fiber: 1g Carbohydrates: 7g Sugar: 3g

143.   Chicken Piccata

Preparation time: 15 minutes
Cooking time: 6 hours
Servings: 4

Ingredients:

- 2 large (6-ounce) boneless, skinless chicken breasts, cut horizontally into skinny slices
- 1 cup all-purpose flour
- 1 tablespoon olive oil
- 1/4 cup lemon juice
- 3 tablespoons nonpareil capers
- 3/4 cup chicken stock
- 1/4 teaspoon freshly ground black pepper

Directions:

1. Dredge both sides of the chicken breast slices in the flour. Discard leftover flour. Heat olive oil in a nonstick pan over medium-high heat. Quickly sear the chicken on both sides to brown, approximately 1 minute per side.
2. Place the chicken, lemon juice, capers, stock, and pepper into a greased 4- to 5-quart slow cooker. Cook on high within 2–3 hours or low for 4–6 hours until the chicken is cooked through and the sauce has thickened.

Nutrition: Calories: 260 Fat: 6.5g Protein: 22g Sodium: 356mg Fiber: 1g Carbohydrates: 27g Sugar: 1g

144.   Pesto Chicken

Preparation time: 15 minutes
Cooking time: 8 hours
Servings: 4

Ingredients:

- 2 pounds boneless, skinless chicken thighs
- 4 medium red potatoes, peeled and diced
- 1-pint cherry tomatoes
- 1/2 cup prepared pesto
- 1/2 teaspoon ground black pepper
- 1/2 teaspoon kosher salt

Directions:

1. Place all ingredients in a greased 4- to 5-quart slow cooker. Cook on high for 3–4 hours or on low for 6–8 hours until chicken is tender. Serve.

Nutrition: Calories: 296 Fat: 5g Protein: 26g Sodium: 407mg Fiber: 4.5g Carbohydrates: 34g Sugar: 4g

145.   Chicken Ragu

Preparation time: 15 minutes
Cooking time: 6 hours
Servings: 6

Ingredients:

- 1-pound boneless skinless chicken breasts, finely chopped
- 3 shallots, finely minced
- 4 cups marinara sauce
- 2 teaspoons crushed rosemary
- 2 cloves garlic, minced
- 1/2 teaspoon freshly ground pepper
- 1/2 teaspoon oregano

Directions:

1. Place all the fixing into a 4- to 5-quart slow cooker. Stir. Cook on low for 4–6 hours. Stir before serving.

Nutrition: Calories: 247 Fat: 6.5g Protein: 19g Sodium: 771mg Fiber: 5g Carbohydrates: 27g Sugar: 16g

146.   Spiced Chicken with Pancetta

Preparation time: 15 minutes
Cooking time: 6 hours
Servings: 6

Ingredients:

- 2 ounces pancetta or prosciutto, chopped
- 6 whole cloves
- 4 garlic cloves, chopped
- 3 fresh sage leaves, chopped
- 1 teaspoon chopped fresh rosemary
- 4 pounds bone-in chicken breasts, legs, or thighs
- salt
- 1 teaspoon coarsely ground pepper
- ¼ cup chicken broth

Directions:

1. Spray the insert of a slow cooker using a nonstick cooking spray. Scatter half of the pancetta, 3 of the cloves, and half the garlic, sage, and rosemary in the cooker.
2. Sprinkle the chicken with salt plus pepper to taste. Place it in the slow cooker. Scatter the remaining pancetta, cloves, garlic, sage, and rosemary over the chicken and add the pepper. Pour in the broth. Cover and cook on low within 4 to 6 hours, then serve.

Nutrition: Calories: 369 Carbs: 4g Fat: 19g Protein: 44g

147. Crunchy Mustard Chicken Diable

Preparation time: 15 minutes
Cooking time: hours
Servings: 6

Ingredients:
- ¼ cup Dijon mustard
- 2 tablespoons chopped shallots or scallions
- ½ teaspoon dried thyme
- 1/8 teaspoon cayenne pepper
- salt
- 4 pounds bone-in chicken thighs, skinned
- 2 tablespoons unsalted butter
- ¾ cup fresh bread crumbs, made from French bread, or panko

Directions:
1. Spray the insert of a slow cooker with nonstick cooking spray. In a small bowl, stir the mustard, shallots, thyme, cayenne, and ½ teaspoon salt. Brush the chicken pieces with the mixture, turning to coat all sides. Place the chicken in the cooker. Cover and cook on low within 4 to 6 hours.
2. Meanwhile, melt the butter in a large skillet. Put the bread crumbs and a bit of salt. Cook over medium heat, occasionally stirring, for 5 minutes, or until the crumbs are lightly toasted. Place the chicken pieces on a platter. Sprinkle with the crumb mixture, patting it on so that it adheres. Serve hot or cold.

Nutrition: Calories: 320 Carbs: 23g Fat: 18g Protein: 15g

148. Spicy Chicken with Green Olives

Preparation time: 15 minutes
Cooking time: 6 hours & 30 minutes
Servings: 6

Ingredients:
- 4 pounds bone-in chicken breasts, legs, or thighs
- salt and freshly ground pepper
- 2 tablespoons olive oil
- 1 medium onion, chopped
- 2 garlic cloves, minced
- 2 teaspoons freshly grated ginger
- 1 teaspoon ground cumin
- 1 teaspoon Spanish smoked paprika
- ¼ teaspoon ground cinnamon
- ¼ teaspoon ground turmeric
- ¼ cup chicken broth or vegetable broth
- 1 cup small pitted green olives, drained
- ½ cup chopped fresh cilantro or mint

Directions:
1. Oiled the bottom of a slow cooker with nonstick cooking spray. Flavor the chicken with salt and pepper to taste, then put the pieces in the slow cooker.
2. Warm-up the oil over medium heat in a medium skillet, add the onion and cook within 5 minutes until slightly softened. Add the garlic, ginger, cumin, paprika, cinnamon, turmeric, and broth and bring to a simmer. Cook for 5 minutes more. Pour the mixture over the chicken.
3. Cover and cook on low within 4 to 6 hours. Rinse the olives and drain well. Add the olives to the cooker and cook for 30 minutes more. With a slotted spoon, transfer the chicken and olives to a serving platter. Cover and keep warm.
4. Pour the liquid into a small saucepan. Simmer until slightly reduced. Taste for seasonings. Spoon the sauce over the chicken. Sprinkle with the herbs and serve hot.

Nutrition: Calories: 239 Carbs: 10g Fat: 10g Protein: 27g

149. Jugged-Chicken

Preparation time: 15 minutes
Cooking time: hours
Servings: 6

Ingredients:
- 4 pounds bone-in chicken breasts, legs, or thighs
- salt and freshly ground pepper
- 1 cup frozen pearl onions, thawed
- 4 ounces prosciutto or pancetta, finely chopped
- 4 garlic cloves, chopped
- 2 bay leaves
- 2 cups canned crushed tomatoes
- ½ cup port wine (tawny or ruby)
- 1 tablespoon Dijon mustard
- chopped fresh flat-leaf parsley

Directions:
1. Sprinkle the chicken with salt plus pepper to taste. Place the pieces in a large slow cooker. Scatter the onions, prosciutto, garlic, and bay leaves on top. Stir the tomatoes, port, Dijon, ½ teaspoon salt, and pepper to taste. Pour the sauce over the chicken. Cover and cook on low within n 4 to 6 hours. Sprinkle with the parsley. Serve hot with rice.

Nutrition: Calories: 240 Carbs: 0g Fat: 20g Protein: 15g

150. Balsamic Chicken with Capers

Preparation time: 15 minutes
Cooking time: 6 hours
Servings: 6

Ingredients:

- ½ cup balsamic vinegar
- 2 tablespoons Dijon mustard
- 2 large garlic cloves, finely chopped
- 1 tablespoon chopped fresh rosemary
- 2 tablespoons drained capers, chopped
- salt and freshly ground pepper
- 4 pounds bone-in chicken breasts, legs, or thighs

Directions:

1. Spray the insert of a large slow cooker with nonstick cooking spray. Mix the vinegar, mustard, garlic, rosemary, capers, ½ teaspoon salt, plus pepper to taste in a medium bowl.
2. Soak the chicken pieces into the batter, turning to coat on all sides. Place the chicken in the cooker and pour it on any remaining coating. Cover and cook on low within 4 to 6 hours. Serve hot.

Nutrition: Calories: 181 Carbs: 13g Fat: 3g Protein: 25g

151. Chicken Tagine

Preparation time: 15 minutes
Cooking time: 6 hours
Servings: 8

Ingredients:

- 3 preserved lemon halves
- 1 medium onion, finely chopped
- 2 garlic cloves, finely chopped
- 1 cup chopped fresh tomatoes or canned tomatoes
- ½ cup chopped fresh cilantro
- 1 teaspoon Spanish smoked paprika
- ½ teaspoon ground cumin
- ½ cup of chicken broth or water
- 2 tablespoons olive oil
- 2 pounds Yukon gold potatoes, cut into ¼-inch-thick slices
- 4 pounds bone-in chicken breasts, legs, or thighs (legs and thighs skinned if you like)
- salt and freshly ground pepper

Directions:

1. Grease the inside of your slow cooker using a nonstick cooking spray. Rinse the preserved lemon halves and pat dry. Scoop the pulp out of the lemons and chop it finely. Reserve the lemon peel.
2. Place the lemon pulp in a medium bowl with the onion, garlic, tomatoes, ¼ cup of the cilantro, paprika, cumin, broth, and olive oil.
3. Put the potatoes, then add half of the lemon mixture. Toss well. Massage the chicken with salt and pepper to taste. Put the chicken over the potatoes and sprinkle with the remaining lemon mixture.
4. Cover and cook on low within 5 to 6 hours. Transfer the cooked chicken plus potatoes to a platter with a slotted spoon. Keep warm. If there is excess liquid in the cooker, pour it into a saucepan and simmer it until reduced.
5. Put the sauce on the chicken plus potatoes and sprinkle with the reserved lemon peel and the remaining ¼ cup cilantro. Serve hot.

Nutrition: Calories: 286 Carbs: 19g Fat: 10g Protein: 30g

152. Chicken with Chorizo, Red Wine, and Roasted Peppers

Preparation time: 15 minutes
Cooking time: 6 hours
Servings: 6

Ingredients:

- 4 pounds bone-in chicken thighs, skinned
- salt and freshly ground pepper
- 8 ounces fully cooked chorizo sausage
- 1 bay leaf
- 2 tablespoons olive oil
- 1 medium onion, chopped
- 1 garlic clove, minced
- ½ cup dry red wine
- ½ teaspoon chopped fresh thyme
- 1 roasted red pepper, thin strips (about 1 cup)
- 2 tablespoons chopped fresh flat-leaf parsley

Directions:

1. Grease the bottom of a slow cooker with nonstick cooking spray. Sprinkle the chicken with salt and pepper. Place the pieces in the cooker, along with the chorizo and bay leaf.
2. In a medium skillet, heat the oil over medium heat. Add the onion, then cook for 10 minutes, or until tender. Stir in the garlic and cook for 1 minute more. Put the red wine and simmer. Stir in the thyme.
3. Scrape the mixture over the chicken and chorizo. Cover and cook on low within 4 to 6 hours. Remove the chorizo and cut into thick slices. Return the chorizo to the slow cooker along with the roasted pepper. Cook on low for 30 minutes more. Discard the bay leaf. Sprinkle with the parsley and serve hot.

Nutrition: Calories: 158 Carbs: 3g Fat: 14g Protein: 4g

153. Chicken with Feta and Tomatoes

Preparation time: 15 minutes
Cooking time: 6 hours & 30 minutes
Servings: 6

Ingredients:
- 4 pounds bone-in chicken breasts, legs, or thighs
- salt and freshly ground pepper
- 2 garlic cloves, finely chopped
- ½ teaspoon dried oregano
- 1-pint cherry or grape tomatoes halved
- ½ cup chicken broth
- ½ cup chopped pitted Kalamata olives
- ½ cup crumbled feta cheese

Directions:
1. Sprinkle the chicken with salt plus pepper. Place the pieces in the slow cooker, overlapping slightly. Scatter the garlic and oregano over the top. Add the tomatoes and broth.
2. Cover and cook on low within 4 to 6 hours. Add the olives and cheese. Cover and cook on low for 15 to 30 minutes more or until hot. Serve hot.

Nutrition: Calories: 236 Carbs: 3g Fat: 7g Protein: 36g

154. Chicken Legs with Sausage, Tomatoes, and Black Olives

Preparation time: 15 minutes
Cooking time: 6 hours
Servings: 6

Ingredients:
- 2 tablespoons olive oil
- 6 sweet Italian sausages (about 1 pound)
- 1 medium onion, chopped
- 2 garlic cloves, finely chopped
- Pinch of crushed red pepper
- ½ cup dry red wine
- 1 28-ounce can crush tomatoes
- 6 whole chicken legs
- salt and freshly ground pepper
- 1 cup pitted black olives
- 3 tablespoons chopped fresh flat-leaf parsley

Directions:
1. Warm-up oil over medium heat in a large skillet, then put the sausages and brown it within 10 minutes. Transfer the sausages to a large slow cooker. Put the onion in the skillet, and cook, often stirring, until softened. Mix in the garlic plus crushed red pepper. Add the wine and simmer. Cook for 1 minute.
2. Pour the skillet contents into the slow cooker. Add the tomatoes and stir. Massage the chicken pieces with salt plus pepper to taste.
3. Place the chicken in the cooker, spooning the sauce over the top. Cover and cook on low within 4 to 6 hours. Stir in the olives. Taste for seasonings. Serve the chicken, sausages, and sauce hot, sprinkled with the parsley.

Nutrition: Calories: 212 Carbs: 8g Fat: 10g Protein: 21g

155. Za'atar Roast Chicken and Vegetables

Preparation time: 15 minutes
Cooking time: 6 hours
Servings: 4

Ingredients:
- 2 medium red onions, sliced
- 1-pound boiling potatoes, such as Yukon gold, thickly sliced
- 3 garlic cloves, finely chopped
- 2 tablespoons za'atar
- salt and freshly ground pepper
- ½ cup chicken broth
- 1 4-pound chicken
- 1 cup cherry or grape tomatoes, halved

Directions:
1. Grease the inside of a slow cooker using a nonstick cooking spray. Scatter the onions, potatoes, and a little of the garlic in the slow cooker. Sprinkle with a bit of the za'atar and salt and pepper to taste. Add the broth.
2. Remove the neck plus giblets from the chicken cavity and reserve them for another use. Trim away any excess fat. Massage and sprinkle the chicken inside and out with the remaining garlic, the remaining za'atar, and salt and pepper to taste.
3. Put the chicken over the vegetables in the cooker. Scatter the tomatoes around the chicken. Cover and cook on low within 5 to 6 hours. Slice the chicken and serve it hot, with the vegetables.

Nutrition: Calories: 266 Carbs: 11g Fat: 23g Protein: 8g

156.   Roast Chicken with Tapenade

Preparation time: 15 minutes
Cooking time: 6 hours
Servings: 4

Ingredients:

- 2 teaspoons chopped fresh rosemary
- 3 large garlic cloves
- ¼ cup store-bought tapenade
- 2 pounds sliced boiling potatoes, such as Yukon gold
- salt and freshly ground pepper
- 1 4-pound chicken

Directions:

1. Grease the inside of a slow cooker using a nonstick cooking spray. Chop the rosemary and garlic. Stir half of the mixture into the tapenade. Put the potatoes in the slow cooker and sprinkle them with the remaining garlic and rosemary and salt and pepper to taste. Toss well.
2. Remove the neck plus giblets from the chicken cavity, then set aside for another use. Trim away any excess fat. Flavor the chicken inside and out with salt and pepper. Place about half of the tapenade mixture inside the chicken cavity.
3. Put the rest of the tapenade on the chicken. Place the chicken on the potatoes in the cooker. Cover and cook on low within 5 to 6 hours. Cut the chicken into pieces and serve hot, with the potatoes.

Nutrition: Calories: 279 Carbs: 4g Fat: 9g Protein: 43g

157.   Chicken with Middle Eastern Pesto

Preparation time: 15 minutes
Cooking time: 6 hours
Servings: 6

Ingredients:

- 1 medium onion, chopped
- 1 medium zucchini, chopped
- ½ cup chicken broth
- 2 preserved lemons or 1 teaspoon grated lemon zest
- 2 garlic cloves
- ½ cup chopped fresh cilantro
- 1 teaspoon ground cumin
- 1 teaspoon Spanish smoked paprika
- ½ teaspoon freshly ground pepper
- 2 tablespoons olive oil
- 1 4-pound chicken

Directions:

1. Grease the large slow cooker with nonstick cooking spray. Scatter the onion and zucchini in the cooker. Add the chicken broth.
2. Rinse the lemons and cut them in half. Scoop out the pulp and discard it. Coarsely chop the lemon skins. Process using a food processor with the garlic, cilantro, cumin, paprika, pepper, and oil. Process until smooth.
3. Remove the neck and giblets, reserve them for another use. Trim away any excess fat. Slide your fingers between the skin and the flesh of the chicken to loosen it. Spread the pesto between the skin and the flesh.
4. Place a little of the pesto inside the chicken. Put the chicken in your slow cooker on top of the vegetables. Cover and cook on low within 4 to 6 hours. Serve hot.

Nutrition: Calories: 254 Carbs: 12g Fat: 9g Protein: 29g

158.   Turkey Breast with Lemon, Capers, and Sage

Preparation time: 15 minutes
Cooking time: 3 hours
Servings: 6

Ingredients:

- 2 large carrots, peeled and sliced
- 1 large onion, sliced
- 1 celery rib, sliced
- 3 tablespoons unsalted butter, softened
- 6 sage leaves, chopped
- 1 teaspoon grated lemon zest
- salt and freshly ground pepper
- 1 boneless turkey breast half
- ½ cup dry white wine or chicken broth
- 1 tablespoon cornstarch, blended with 3 tablespoons water
- 2 tablespoons capers, rinsed, drained, and chopped
- 1 tablespoon chopped fresh flat-leaf parsley
- 1–2 tablespoons fresh lemon juice

Directions:

1. Grease the inside of a slow cooker using a nonstick cooking spray. Scatter the carrots, onion, and celery in the slow cooker. Blend 2 tablespoons of the butter and the sage, lemon zest, salt, and pepper to taste. Loosen the turkey breast skin, then gently spread the butter mixture inside the skin and meat.
2. Put the turkey breast in your slow cooker. Pour the wine around the turkey. Cover and cook on

high within 2 to 3 hours. Remove the turkey from the pot. Cover and keep warm, then drain the cooking liquid into a saucepan. Bring the juices to a boil.

3. Add the cornstarch mixture to the turkey juices and stir well. Cook within 1 minute. Turn off the heat, mix in the remaining 1 tablespoon butter, the capers, parsley, and lemon juice to taste. Carve the turkey and serve it hot, with the sauce.

Nutrition: Calories: 181 Carbs: 13g Fat: 3g Protein: 25g

159. Turkey Meatloaf with Sun-Dried Tomatoes and Mozzarella

Preparation time: 15 minutes
Cooking time: 4 hours
Servings: 8

Ingredients:
- 1 cup drained sun-dried tomatoes in oil
- 2 pounds ground turkey
- 3 large eggs, beaten
- ½ cup plain dry bread crumbs
- ½ cup finely chopped scallions
- ½ cup freshly grated Parmigiano-Reggiano
- ¼ cup chopped fresh basil
- 1½ teaspoons salt
- freshly ground pepper
- 8 ounces mozzarella, cut into ½-inch cubes

Directions:
1. Place a foil into the insert of a large slow cooker, pressing it against the bottom and up the sides. Spray the foil and the insert with nonstick cooking spray.
2. Rinse the sun-dried tomatoes under warm water. Pat them dry with paper towels. Set aside a few pieces for the top of the meatloaf. Stack the remaining tomatoes and chop them into small pieces.
3. Mix all the fixings except the mozzarella and reserved sun-dried tomatoes in a large bowl. Add the mozzarella. Shape the batter into an oval loaf slightly smaller than the interior of the slow cooker.
4. Carefully place the loaf into the cooker on top of the foil. Press the reserved tomato pieces into the top in a decorative pattern. Cover and cook on high within 3 to 4 hours. Carefully lift the meatloaf out of the slow cooker. Slide the meatloaf onto a serving platter. Cut into slices and serve hot.

Nutrition: Calories: 388 Carbs: 28g Fat: 18g Protein: 30g

160. Duck Ragu

Preparation time: 15 minutes
Cooking time: 5 hours
Servings: 8

Ingredients:
- 2 tablespoons olive oil
- 4 ounces pancetta, chopped
- 6 whole duck legs and thighs, skinned
- salt and freshly ground pepper
- 4 medium carrots, peeled and chopped
- 2 celery ribs, chopped
- 1 large red onion, chopped
- 2 tablespoons all-purpose flour
- 1 cup dry red wine
- ½ cup tomato paste
- Pinch of ground cloves
- 2 cups chicken broth

Directions:
1. Warm-up, oil over medium heat in a large skillet, then put the pancetta and cook, often stirring, until nicely browned, about 10 minutes. Remove the pancetta to a large slow cooker.
2. Pat the duck legs dry with paper towels. Flavor it all over with salt and pepper. Add the duck legs to the skillet, batches if necessary, and cook until browned on all sides, about 15 minutes in all.
3. Transfer the duck to the cooker. Put the carrots, celery, and onion in the skillet. Cook for 10 minutes, or until the vegetables are tender. Stir in the flour and cook within 1 minute. Add the wine, tomato paste, and cloves and cook, scraping the pan's bottom until the liquid comes to a boil.
4. Scrape the mixture into the slow cooker. Add the broth. Cover and cook on low within 4 to 5 hours, or until the duck is very tender and coming away from the bone.
5. Remove the duck legs, then put it on a cutting board, but leave the cooker on. Cut it into small dice. Discard the bones. Move back the duck meat to the sauce and reheat. Serve hot.

Nutrition: Calories: 144 Carbs: 4g Fat: 4g Protein: 4g

161.   Beef Stew with Eggplants

Preparation time: 15 minutes
Cooking time: 10 hours
Servings: 2

Ingredients:

- 10 oz. of the beef neck, or another tender cut, chopped into bite-sized pieces
- 1 large eggplant, sliced
- 2 cups of fire-roasted tomatoes
- ½ cup of fresh green peas
- 1 cup of beef broth
- 4 tbsp. of olive oil
- 2 tbsp. of tomato paste
- 1 tbsp. of Cayenne pepper, ground
- ½ tsp of chili pepper, ground (optional)
- ½ tsp of salt
- Parmesan cheese

Directions:

1. Grease the bottom of a slow cooker with olive oil. Toss all ingredients in it and add about 1-1 ½ cup of water. Cook within 8-10 hours on low, or until the meat is fork-tender. Sprinkle with Parmesan cheese before serving, but this is optional.

Nutrition: Calories 195 Proteins 15.3g Carbohydrates 9.6g Fat 11.1g

162.   Chopped Veal Kebab

Preparation time: 15 minutes
Cooking time: 10 hours
Servings: 5

Ingredients:

- 2 lb. boneless veal shoulder, cut into bite-sized pieces
- 3 large tomatoes, roughly chopped
- 2 tbsp. of all-purpose flour
- 3 tbsp. of butter
- 1 tbsp. of cayenne pepper
- 1 tsp of salt
- 1 tbsp. of parsley, finely chopped
- 1 cup of Greek yogurt (can be replaced with sour cream), for serving
- 1 pide bread (can be replaced with any bread you have on hand)

Directions:

1. Oil the bottom of your slow cooker with one tablespoon of butter. Make a layer with veal chops

and pour enough water to cover. Season with salt and close the lid. Set to low and simmer within 8-10 hours. Remove, then transfer to a plate.

2. Dissolve the rest of the butter in a small skillet. Add one tablespoon of cayenne pepper, two tablespoons of all-purpose flour, and briefly stir-fry - for about two minutes. Remove from the heat.

3. Chop pide bread and arrange on a serving plate. Place the meat and tomato on top. Drizzle with browned cayenne pepper, top with Greek yogurt, and sprinkle with chopped parsley. Serve immediately.

Nutrition: Calories 437 Proteins 49.7g Carbohydrates 8.9g Fat 21.8g

163.   Garlic Meatballs

Preparation time: 15 minutes
Cooking time: 8 hours
Servings: 5

Ingredients:

- 1 lb. lean ground beef
- 7 oz rice
- 2 small onions, peeled and finely chopped
- 2 garlic cloves, crushed
- 1 egg, beaten
- 1 large potato, peeled and sliced
- 3 tbsp. of extra virgin olive oil
- 1 tsp of salt

Directions:

1. Mix the lean ground beef with rice, finely chopped onions, crushed garlic, one beaten egg, and salt in a large bowl. Shape the batter into 15-20 meatballs.

2. Oiled the bottom of your slow cooker with three tablespoons of olive oil. Make the first layer with sliced potatoes and top with meatballs. Cook low within for 6-8 hours.

Nutrition: Calories 468 Proteins 33g Carbohydrates 47g Fat 15.3g

164. Meat Pie with Yogurt

Preparation time: 15 minutes
Cooking time: 6 hours
Servings: 6

Ingredients:
- 2 lb. lean ground beef
- 5-6 garlic cloves, crushed
- 1 tsp of salt
- ½ tsp freshly ground black pepper
- 1 (16 oz.) pack yufka dough
- ½ cup of butter, melted
- 1 cup of sour cream
- 3 cups of liquid yogurt

Directions:
1. Mix the ground beef with garlic cloves, salt, and pepper in a large bowl. Mix well until fully incorporated. Lay a sheet of yufka on a work surface and brush with melted butter. Line with the meat mixture and roll-up. Repeat the process until all fixing is used.
2. Gently place in a lightly greased slow cooker and close the lid. Cook for 4-6 hours on low, remove from the cooker, and allow it to cool. Meanwhile, combine sour cream with yogurt. Spread the mixture over the pie and serve cold.

Nutrition: Calories 503 Proteins 47.4g Carbohydrates 2.6g Fat 32.8g

165. Moussaka

Preparation time: 15 minutes
Cooking time: 8 hours
Servings: 5

Ingredients:
- 2 lb. large potatoes, peeled and sliced
- 1 lb. lean ground beef
- 1 large onion, peeled and finely chopped
- 1 tsp of salt
- ½ tsp of black pepper, ground
- ½ cup of milk
- 2 large eggs, beaten
- Vegetable oil
- Sour cream or Greek yogurt, for serving

Directions:
1. Grease the bottom of your cooker with some vegetable oil. Make one layer with sliced potatoes and brush with some milk. Spread the ground beef and make another layer with potatoes. Brush with the remaining milk, add ½ cup of water and close the lid.
2. Cook within 8 hours on low or 4-6 hours on high. When done, make the final layer with a beaten egg.

Cover the cooker and let it stand for about 10 minutes. Top with some sour cream or Greek yogurt and serve!

Nutrition: Calories 458 Proteins 34.9g Carbohydrates 36g Fat 19.2g

166. Pepper Meat

Preparation time: 15 minutes
Cooking time: 10 hours
Servings: 6

Ingredients:
- 2 lbs. of beef fillet or another tender cut
- 5 medium-sized onions, peeled and finely chopped
- 3 tbsp. of tomato paste
- 2 tbsp. of oil
- 1 tbsp. of butter, melted
- 2 tbsp. of fresh parsley, finely chopped
- ½ tsp of freshly ground black pepper
- 1 tsp of salt

Directions:
1. Oiled the bottom of your slow cooker with some oil. About two tablespoons will be enough. Slice the meat into bite-sized and place them in the cooker.
2. Add finely chopped onions, tomato paste, fresh parsley, salt, and pepper. Mix and put about 2 cups of water. Cook on low for 8-10 hours. Stir in one tablespoon of melted butter and serve warm.

Nutrition: Calories 382 Proteins 47.3g Carbohydrates 10.3g Fat 16g

167. Roast Lamb

Preparation time: 15 minutes
Cooking time: 8 hours
Servings: 5

Ingredients:
- 2 lb. lamb leg
- 3 tbsp. extra virgin olive oil
- 2 tsp salt

Directions:
1. Grease the bottom of a slow cooker with three tablespoons of olive oil. Rinse and generously season the meat with salt and place in the cooker. Cook on low within one hour on high and 6-7 hours on low, or until the meat is tender and separates from the bones.

Nutrition: Calories 473 Proteins 49.7g Carbohydrates 8.9g Fat 21.8g

168. Rosemary Meatballs

Preparation time: 15 minutes
Cooking time: 6 hours
Servings: 5

Ingredients:
- 1 lb. lean ground beef
- 3 garlic cloves, crushed
- ¼ cup of all-purpose flour
- 1 tbsp. of fresh rosemary, crushed
- 1 large egg, beaten
- ½ tsp of salt
- 3 tbsp. of extra virgin olive oil

For serving:
- 2 cups of liquid yogurt
- 1 cup of Greek yogurt
- 2 tbsp. of fresh parsley
- 1 garlic clove, crushed

Directions:
1. Mix the ground beef with crushed garlic, rosemary, one egg, and salt in a large bowl. Lightly dampen hands and shape 1 ½ inch balls transferring into the greased cooker as you work. Slowly add about ½ cup of water.
2. Cook on low for 4-6 hours. Remove from the cooker and cool completely. Meanwhile, combine liquid yogurt with Greek yogurt, parsley, and crushed garlic. Stir well and drizzle over meatballs.

Nutrition: Calories 477 Proteins 49g Carbohydrates 17.8g Fat 21.4g

169. Spicy White Peas

Preparation time: 15 minutes
Cooking time: 9 hours
Servings: 4

Ingredients:
- 1 lb. of white peas
- 4 slices of bacon
- 1 large onion, finely chopped
- 1 small chili pepper, finely chopped
- 2 tbsp. of all-purpose flour
- 2 tbsp. of butter
- 1 tbsp. of cayenne pepper
- 3 bay leaves, dried
- 1 tsp of salt
- ½ tsp of freshly ground black pepper

Directions:
1. Melt two tablespoons of butter in a slow cooker. Add chopped onion and stir well. Now add bacon, peas, finely chopped chili pepper, bay leaves, salt, and pepper.
2. Gently stir in two tablespoons of flour and add three cups of water. Securely close the lid and cook for 8-9 hours on low setting or 5 hours on high.

Nutrition: Calories 210 Proteins 4g Carbohydrates 24g Fat 12g

170. Stuffed Collard Greens

Preparation time: 15 minutes
Cooking time: 4 hours
Servings: 5

Ingredients:
- 1 1/2 lb. of collard greens, steamed
- 1 lb. lean ground beef
- 2 small onions, peeled and finely chopped
- ½ cup long grain rice
- 2 tbsp. of olive oil
- 1 tsp of salt
- ½ tsp of freshly ground black pepper
- 1 tsp of mint leaves, finely chopped

Directions:
1. Boil a pot of water, then gently put the collard greens. Briefly cook for 2-3 minutes. Drain and gently squeeze the greens and set aside. Mix the ground beef with the chopped onions, rice, salt, pepper, and mint leaves in a large bowl.
2. Oil the slow cooker with some olive oil. Place leaves on your work surface, vein side up. Use one tablespoon of the meat mixture and place it in the bottom center of each leaf.
3. Fold the sides over and roll up tightly. Tuck in the sides and gently transfer to a slow cooker. Cook on low within ten hours, or on high setting for 4 hours.

Nutrition: Calories 156 Proteins 5.2g Carbohydrates 21g Fat 7g

171.   Stuffed Onions

Preparation time: 15 minutes
Cooking time: 8 hours
Servings: 5

Ingredients:

- 10-12 medium-sized sweet onions, peeled
- 1 lb. of lean ground beef
- ½ cup of rice
- 3 tbsp. of olive oil
- 1 tbsp. of dry mint, ground
- 1 tsp of Cayenne pepper, ground
- ½ tsp of cumin, ground
- 1 tsp of salt
- ½ cup of tomato paste
- ½ cup Italian-style bread crumbs
- A handful of fresh parsley, finely chopped

Directions:

1. Cut a ¼-inch slice from the top of each onion and trim a small amount from the bottom end; this will make the onions stand upright. Place onions in a microwave-safe dish and add about one cup of water. Cover with a tight lid and microwave on HIGH 10 to 12 minutes or until onions are tender.
2. Remove onions from a dish and cool slightly. Now carefully remove inner layers of onions with a paring knife, leaving about a ¼-inch onion shell. Mix the ground beef with rice, olive oil, mint, cayenne pepper, cumin, salt, and bread crumbs in a large bowl. Use one tablespoon of the mixture to fill the onions.
3. Grease the bottom of a slow cooker with some oil and add onions. Put 2 ½ cups of water and cover. Cook within 6-8 hours on a low setting. Sprinkle with chopped parsley or even arugula and serve with sour cream and pide bread.

Nutrition: Calories 464 Proteins 34g Carbohydrates 48.4g Fat 15.2g

172.   Veal Okra

Preparation time: 15 minutes
Cooking time: 10 hours
Servings: 4

Ingredients:

- 7 oz. veal shoulder, blade chops
- 1 lb. okra, rinsed and trimmed
- 3 large Jerusalem artichokes, whole
- 2 medium-sized tomatoes, halved
- 2-3 fresh cauliflower florets
- 2 cups of vegetable broth
- A handful of fresh broccoli
- 3 tablespoons of extra virgin olive oil
- 1 tsp of Himalayan salt
- ½ tsp of freshly ground black pepper

Directions:

1. Grease your slow cooker with three tablespoons of olive oil. Set aside. Cut each okra pod in half lengthwise and place in a slow cooker. Add tomato halves, Jerusalem artichokes, cauliflower florets, a handful of fresh broccoli, and top with meat chops.
2. Season with salt and pepper and add two cups of vegetable broth. Give it a good stir and close the lid. Set the heat to low and cook within 8-10 hours.

Nutrition: Calories 281 Proteins 19.6g Carbohydrates 17.4g Fat 15.5g

173.   Winter Lamb Stew

Preparation time: 15 minutes
Cooking time: 10 hours
Servings: 4

Ingredients:

- 1 lb. of lamb neck, boneless
- 2 medium-sized potatoes, peeled and chopped into bite-sized pieces
- 2 large carrots, sliced
- 1 medium-sized tomato, diced
- 1 small red bell pepper, chopped
- 1 garlic head, whole
- A handful of fresh parsley, finely chopped
- 2 tbsp. of extra virgin olive oil
- ¼ cup of lemon juice
- ½ tsp of salt
- ½ tsp of black pepper, ground

Directions:

1. Grease the bottom of a slow cooker with olive oil. Place the meat at the bottom of the cooker and season with salt.
2. Now add the other ingredients, tuck in one garlic head in the middle of the pot and add 2 cups of water. Add a handful of fresh parsley and close the lid. Set the heat to low and simmer for 10 hours.

Nutrition: Calories 379 Proteins 34.6g Carbohydrates 24.2g Fat 15.7g

174.   Beef in Barolo

Preparation time: 15 minutes
Cooking time: 6 hours
Servings: 6

Ingredients:
- 1/3 cup all-purpose flour
- Salt
- ground pepper
- 1 3-pound boneless beef chuck
- 3 tbsp. olive oil
- 2 oz. pancetta, chopped
- 1 onion, chopped
- 2 garlic cloves, chopped
- 1 cup dry red wine
- 2 cups tomatoes, chopped
- 1 cup Meat Broth
- 2 medium carrots, sliced
- 1 medium celery rib, sliced
- 1 bay leaf
- a few grounds clove

Directions:
1. Mix the flour with salt plus pepper, put it on wax paper. Roll the meat in the flour mixture. Warm-up oil on medium-high heat in a large skillet, then put the beef and brown within 15 minutes.
2. Put the meat in a slow cooker. Put the pancetta plus onion in the skillet. Reduce the heat to medium and cook within 10 minutes, occasionally stirring, until the onion is tender. Stir in the garlic. Add the wine and simmer.
3. Pour the batter over the beef. Put the tomatoes and broth. Put the carrots, celery, bay leaf, plus ground cloves around the meat. Cover and cook on low within 6 hours, then move the meat to a platter. Discard the bay leaf, then slice the meat and spoon on the sauce.

Nutrition: Calories: 150 Carbs: 3g Fat: 5g Protein: 19g

175.   Peppery Beef Stew

Preparation time: 15 minutes
Cooking time: 8 hours
Servings: 6

Ingredients:
- ½ cup all-purpose flour
- Salt
- 3 pounds boneless beef chuck, 2-inch chunks
- 3 tablespoons olive oil
- 1 cup dry red wine
- 2 cups canned tomato puree

- 2 garlic cloves, chopped, plus 6 whole garlic cloves, peeled
- 1 tablespoon whole black peppercorns
- ½ teaspoon freshly ground pepper, or to taste

Directions:
1. On a piece of wax paper, stir the flour and salt to taste. Toss the beef with the flour and shake off any excess. Warm-up oil over medium-high heat in a large, heavy skillet, then put the meat in batches, without crowding the pan. Brown the beef well on all sides.
2. Transfer the beef meat to a large slow cooker. Put the wine in the skillet and simmer, scraping the bottom of the pan. Add the tomato puree, garlic, peppercorns, and ground pepper. Cook within 10 minutes.
3. Pour the mixture into the slow cooker. Cook on low within 6 to 8 hours or until the beef is very tender. Taste for seasoning before serving.

Nutrition: Calories: 187 Carbs: 12g Fat: 5g Protein: 23g

176.   Beef Goulash

Preparation time: 15 minutes
Cooking time: 6 hours
Servings: 8

Ingredients:
- 3 tablespoons lard, drippings, or vegetable oil
- 3½ pounds beef chuck, boneless, cut into 2-inch cubes
- Salt and freshly ground pepper
- 4 medium onions, sliced
- 2 garlic cloves, finely chopped
- 1 cup dry red wine
- 2 tablespoons tomato paste
- 1 bay leaf
- ¼ cup sweet paprika
- 1 tablespoon chopped fresh marjoram leaves
- 1 teaspoon ground cumin
- 1 2-inch strip lemon zest
- Juice of ½ lemon

Directions:
1. Heat the lard, drippings in a large skillet over medium-high heat. Pat the meat dry and put in the pan. Cook until browned on all sides. Move the meat to your slow cooker and brown the rest of the meat. Sprinkle the meat with salt and pepper.
2. Adjust the heat to medium, then put the onions in the skillet. Cook, occasionally stirring, until lightly browned. Stir in the garlic. Put the wine plus tomato paste and simmer. Pour the mixture into the slow cooker. Stir in the bay leaf, paprika, marjoram, cumin, and lemon zest.

3. Add enough water to cover the meat barely. Cover and cook on low within 6 hours, or until the beef is very tender when pierced with a fork. Stir in the lemon juice. Remove the bay leaf and lemon zest. Serve hot.

Nutrition: Calories: 272 Carbs: 25g Fat: 7g Protein: 22g

177.   Braised Beef with Anchovies and Rosemary

Preparation time: 15 minutes
Cooking time: 6 hours
Servings: 6

Ingredients:
- 2 tablespoons olive oil
- 4 pounds beef shin or 3 pounds boneless chuck, cut into 2-inch cubes
- 2 ounces pancetta, chopped
- Salt and freshly ground pepper
- 2 large garlic cloves, finely chopped
- 6 anchovy fillets
- 1 cup dry white wine
- 1 3-inch fresh rosemary sprig

Directions:
1. Warm-up oil over medium-high heat in a large, heavy skillet. Pat the beef dry. Add only as much of the beef and pancetta to the pan as will fit comfortably without crowding.
2. Cook, then transfer the meat to a large slow cooker and brown the remaining meat. Rub the meat with salt plus pepper to taste. Discard or spoon off the excess fat from the pan and adjust the heat to medium.
3. Put the garlic and anchovies and cook, stirring, within 2 minutes. Put the wine and bring it to a simmer. Pour the liquid into the slow cooker. Add the rosemary. Cover and cook within low for 6 hours. Discard the rosemary and serve hot.

Nutrition: Calories: 334 Carbs: 0g Fat: 13g Protein: 0g

178.   Braciole in Tomato Sauce

Preparation time: 15 minutes
Cooking time: 4 hours
Servings: 8

Ingredients:
- 2 ½-inch-thick beef round steaks (each about 1 pound)
- Salt and freshly ground pepper
- ½ cup freshly grated Pecorino Romano
- 3 tablespoons chopped fresh parsley
- 4 garlic cloves, finely chopped
- 2 tablespoons olive oil
- 1 large onion, chopped
- 1 28-ounce can tomato puree
- 6 fresh basil leaves, torn into bits

Directions:
1. Put each steak in between two sheets of plastic wrap. Gently pound the steaks with a mallet or the bottom of a small pan to a 1/8-inch thickness. Cut each steak in half.
2. Flavor the meat with salt and pepper to taste, then with the cheese, parsley, and garlic. Roll up each piece of meat. With kitchen twine, tie each roll up like a roast.
3. Warm-up the oil on medium-high heat in a large, heavy skillet. Put the meat rolls and cook until browned on one side. Turn the rolls and scatter the onion around the meat.
4. Cook, then transfer the rolls and onion to a large slow cooker and add the tomato puree and basil. Cover and cook on low within 4 hours, or until the meat is tender. Transfer the meat to a cutting board. Remove the twine, then slice the meat into thick slices. Spoon on the sauce. Serve hot.

Nutrition: Calories: 220 Carbs: 6g Fat: 15g Protein: 14g

179.   Beef Shanks with Red Wine and Tomatoes

Preparation time: 15 minutes
Cooking time: 8 hours
Servings: 8

Ingredients:
- About 20 whole garlic cloves (1 large head), peeled
- 2 cups dry red wine
- 1 14-ounce can Italian peeled tomatoes with their juice, chopped
- 1 4-inch fresh rosemary sprig or 1 tablespoon dried
- 3 pounds bone-in beef shanks, about 2 inches thick, trimmed
- Salt and freshly ground pepper
- Thick-sliced Italian bread

Directions:
1. Scatter the garlic cloves in the slow cooker. Add the wine, tomatoes, and rosemary. Place the beef in the cooker and sprinkle with salt to taste and plenty of pepper.
2. Cover and cook on low within 6 to 8 hours or until the meat is tender and falling off the bone. Skim off the excess fat and taste for seasoning.
3. Toast the bread and place 1 or 2 slices in each serving dish. Crushed the meat up with a spoon

and scoop some of the meat, garlic, and pan juices over the bread. Serve with the marrow bones.

Nutrition: Calories: 479 Carbs: 11g Fat: 17g Protein: 61g

180.   Balsamic-Glazed Short Ribs

Preparation time: 15 minutes
Cooking time: 8 hours
Servings: 6

Ingredients:
- 1 tablespoon olive oil
- 4 5 pounds bone-in beef short ribs, well-trimmed
- Salt and freshly ground pepper
- 2 large garlic cloves, finely chopped
- ½ cup dry red wine
- 1/3 cup balsamic vinegar
- 1 3-inch fresh rosemary sprig

Directions:
1. Warm-up the oil in a large, heavy skillet on medium-high heat. Pat the meat dry and put only as many pieces in the pan as will fit comfortably. Cook, then transfer the meat to a slow cooker. Flavor the ribs with salt plus pepper to taste.
2. Discard all but reserve 1 tablespoon of the fat and adjust the heat to medium. Put the garlic and cook within 1 minute. Add the wine and vinegar and simmer while scraping the bottom of the pan.
3. Put the liquid on the ribs and add the rosemary. Cover and cook on low within 8 hours. Remove the ribs, and discard the rosemary sprig with any loose bones. Skim the fat off the liquid.
4. Pour the rest of all the sauce into a saucepan and cook over medium-high heat until thickened. Put the sauce over the ribs and serve hot.

Nutrition: Calories: 249 Carbs: 0g Fat: 22g Protein: 11g

181.   Roman Oxtail Stew

Preparation time: 15 minutes
Cooking time: 6 hours & 30 minutes
Servings: 6
Ingredients:
- ¼ cup olive oil
- 4 pounds oxtails, about 1½ inches thick
- 1 large onion, chopped
- 2 garlic cloves, chopped
- 1 cup dry red wine
- 1 28-ounce can Italian peeled tomatoes with their juice
- ¼ teaspoon ground cloves
- Salt and freshly ground pepper

- 6 medium celery ribs, sliced
- 1 tablespoon chopped bittersweet chocolate
- 2 tablespoons pine nuts
- 2 tablespoons raisins

Directions:
1. Warm-up oil over medium-high heat in a large skillet. Add the oxtails, in batches if necessary, and brown nicely on all sides. Transfer the oxtails to the slow cooker.
2. Put off all but 2 tablespoons of the fat and lower the heat to medium. Add the onion to the skillet and cook until lightly browned, within 10 minutes. Mix in the garlic and cook within 30 seconds.
3. Put the wine and scrape the bottom of the pan. Stir in the tomatoes, cloves, and salt and pepper to taste. Simmer the liquid, then pour over the oxtails. Cover and cook on low within 6 hours. Boil a large saucepan of water.
4. Add the celery and cook for 1 minute. Drain well. Turn the slow cooker to high. Stir in the chocolate. Add the celery, pine nuts, and raisins. Cook for 30 minutes, or until the flavors blend. Serve hot.

Nutrition: Calories: 233 Carbs: 19g Fat: 12g Protein: 13g

182.   "Big Meatball" Meat Loaf

Preparation time: 15 minutes
Cooking time: hours
Servings: 8

Ingredients:
- 2 pounds ground beef chuck or round
- 3 large eggs, beaten
- 2 garlic cloves, minced
- 1 cup freshly grated Pecorino Romano
- ½ cup plain dry bread crumbs
- ¼ cup chopped fresh parsley
- 1½ teaspoons salt
- Freshly ground pepper
- 2 cups meatless tomato sauce

Directions:
1. Put the foil in a large slow cooker, pressing it against the bottom and up the sides. Mix all the fixing except the tomato sauce in a large bowl. Shape the mixture into a loaf. Carefully place it in the slow cooker on top of the foil.
2. Pour the tomato sauce over the top. Cover and cook on high within 4 hours, or until an instant-read thermometer reads 165° to 170°F. Carefully lift the meatloaf using the ends of the foil as handles. Slide the meatloaf onto a serving platter. Slice and serve.

Nutrition: Calories: 197 Carbs: 8g Fat: 1g Protein: 20g

183.   Springtime Veal Stew

Preparation time: 15 minutes
Cooking time: 4 hours & 35 minutes
Servings: 6

Ingredients:

- 3 large carrots, cut into ¼-inch-thick slices
- 2 medium onions, chopped
- 3 tablespoons olive oil
- 1 garlic clove, finely chopped
- 2 teaspoons chopped fresh rosemary
- 2 pounds veal shoulder or chuck, trimmed and cut into 2-inch pieces
- 2 cups Chicken Broth
- 2 tablespoons tomato paste
- Salt and freshly ground pepper
- 4 cups of water
- 1 cup asparagus, 1-inch pieces
- 1 cup thawed frozen green peas or baby lima beans

Directions:

1. Scatter the carrot slices in a large slow cooker. Cook the onions in the oil over medium heat until softened, about 10 minutes in a large skillet. Stir in the garlic and rosemary. Put the veal and cook, occasionally stirring, until the meat is no longer pink. Scrape the veal mixture into the slow cooker.
2. Move back the skillet to the heat and add the broth and tomato paste. Cook until the liquid comes to a simmer, then pour into the slow cooker. Put a pinch of salt plus pepper to taste. Cover and cook on low within 4 hours, or until the veal is tender when pierced with a fork. Boil the water in a medium saucepan.
3. Add the asparagus and salt to taste. Simmer within 3 to 5 minutes, depending on the thickness, until crisp-tender. Drain well. Add the asparagus and the peas or beans to the slow cooker. Cover and cook within 30 minutes more. Serve hot.

Nutrition: Calories: 280 Carbs: 31g Fat: 4g Protein: 32g

184.   Osso Buco with Red

Preparation time: 15 minutes
Cooking time: 5 hours
Servings: 6

Ingredients:

- 6 1½-inch-thick slices veal shank
- ¼ cup all-purpose flour
- Salt and freshly ground pepper
- 2 tablespoons unsalted butter
- 1 tablespoon olive oil
- 2 medium carrots, chopped
- 1 medium onion, chopped
- 1 medium celery rib, chopped
- 1 cup dry red wine
- 1 cup peeled, seeded, and chopped fresh tomatoes
- 1 cup Meat Broth
- 2 teaspoons chopped fresh thyme or ½ teaspoon dried

Directions:

1. To help hold the shape of the meat as it cooks, ties a piece of kitchen twine around the circumference of each shank. On a piece of wax paper, stir the flour and salt and pepper to taste. In a large skillet, melt the butter with the oil over medium heat.
2. Dip the cut sides of each piece of meat in the flour mixture and place it in the skillet, in batches if necessary. Cook, turning the meat once until nicely browned, about 10 minutes on each side.
3. Moved the cooked meat to your slow cooker. Add the chopped vegetables to the skillet. Cook, occasionally stirring, until golden brown, about 15 minutes.
4. Put the wine in the skillet, then cook, scraping the bottom of the pan, until the liquid comes to a boil. Stir in the tomatoes, broth, and thyme. Pour the sauce over the veal. Cover and cook on low within 4 to 5 hours. Remove the twine and serve hot.

Nutrition: Calories: 256 Carbs: 14g Fat: 14g Protein: 19g

185.   Milk-Braised Pork Loin

Preparation time: 15 minutes
Cooking time: hours
Servings: 8

Ingredients:

- 3 pounds boneless pork loin, rolled and tied
- Salt and freshly ground pepper
- 2 tablespoons unsalted butter
- 1 tablespoon olive oil
- 2 medium carrots, finely chopped
- 1 medium onion, finely chopped
- 1 medium celery rib, finely chopped
- 2 cups whole milk

Directions:

1. Pat the meat dry with paper towels. Sprinkle it with salt plus pepper. Dissolve the butter with the oil in a large, heavy skillet over medium-high heat. Cook the meat on one side. Flip it over and put the vegetables around the meat. Cook, then transfer the meat to the slow cooker.
2. Add the milk to the skillet with the vegetables and bring it to a simmer. Pour the contents of the skillet over the meat.

3. Cover and cook on low within 3 to 4 hours. If the sauce is too thin, pour it into a saucepan and reduce it over medium heat. Remove the twine from the meat. Slice the meat, then arrange it on a platter. Spoon the sauce down the center and serve hot.

Nutrition: Calories: 190 Carbs: 8g Fat: 6g Protein: 25g

186.   Pork Chops with Fennel Seeds

Preparation time: 15 minutes
Cooking time: 8 hours
Servings: 6

Ingredients:
- 6 bone-in pork rib chops (about 3½ pounds total)
- Salt and freshly ground pepper
- 2 tablespoons olive oil
- 2 large onions, thinly sliced
- ½ cup dry white wine
- 1 tablespoon fennel seeds
- 1 cup Meat Broth

Directions:
1. Pat dry the pork chops and sprinkle them on both sides with salt and pepper to taste. Warm-up oil over medium-high heat in a large, heavy skillet. Add as many of the chops as will fit in the pan without touching. Cook, turning the chops occasionally until nicely browned on all sides.
2. Put the cooked chops in your slow cooker. Brown the remaining pork chops. Add the onions to the skillet, reduce the heat to medium, and cook for about 10 minutes. Stir in the wine and fennel seeds and bring it to a simmer.
3. Put the broth, then scrape the bottom of the pan until boiling. Pour the mixture over the chops. Cover and cook on low heat within 6 to 8 hours. Serve hot.

Nutrition: Calories: 176 Carbs: 313g Fat: 7g Protein: 14g

187.   Pork Stew Agrodolce

Preparation time: 15 minutes
Cooking time: 6 hours
Servings: 8

Ingredients:
- 3 pounds boneless pork shoulder, 2-inch pieces
- Salt and freshly ground pepper
- 3 tablespoons olive oil
- 3 large onions, chopped

- 2 large celery ribs, chopped
- 1 cup dry white wine
- 3 tablespoons balsamic vinegar
- 3 large carrots, cut into 1-inch chunks
- ½ cup golden raisins

Directions:
1. Pat the pork dries with paper towels. Sprinkle the meat with salt and pepper. Warm-up oil over medium-high heat in a large, heavy skillet.
2. Put the pork, then brown all sides and move back it to the slow cooker. Reduce the heat to medium. Put the onions plus celery in the skillet and cook until golden.
3. Put the wine and vinegar, then simmer. Transfer the onion batter to the slow cooker. Put the carrots and raisins. Cover and cook on low within 6 hours. Serve hot.

Nutrition: Calories: 190 Carbs: 0g Fat: 10g Protein: 23g

188.   Country-Style Pork Ribs with Tomato and Peppers

Preparation time: 15 minutes
Cooking time: hours
Servings: 6

Ingredients:
- 4 pounds country-style pork ribs
- Salt and freshly ground pepper
- 2 tablespoons olive oil
- 2 medium onions, chopped
- 2 large garlic cloves, chopped
- ½ cup dry white wine
- 2 tablespoons tomato paste
- 1 cup canned tomato puree
- 1 teaspoon dried oregano
- 4 medium red bell peppers, ½-inch slices

Directions:
1. Pat dry the ribs, then flavor them with salt plus pepper. Warm-up oil over medium heat in a large skillet. Put the ribs in the pan without touching. Cook the meat, flipping it occasionally. Put the cooked ribs in the slow cooker and brown the remaining ribs.
2. Put the onions plus garlic in the skillet and cook within 5 minutes. Mix in the wine plus tomato paste and cook until it simmers. Mix in the tomato puree, oregano, plus salt and pepper to taste.
3. Remove, then scatter the peppers over the pork in the slow cooker. Pour on the sauce. Cover and cook on low within 6 hours. Remove any loose bones and skim off the fat. Serve hot.

Nutrition: Calories: 240 Carbs: 0g Fat: 18g Protein: 18g

189.   Balsamic Brussels Sprouts

Preparation Time: 10 minutes
Cooking Time: 4 hours and 10 minutes
Servings: 6

Ingredients:
- 2 tablespoons brown sugar
- ½ cup balsamic vinegar
- 2 lb. Brussels sprouts, trimmed and sliced in half
- 2 tablespoons olive oil
- 2 tablespoons butter, cut into cubes
- Salt and pepper to taste
- ¼ cup Parmesan cheese, grated

Directions:
1. Put the brown sugar and vinegar in a saucepan over medium heat. Mix and bring to a boil. Reduce heat and simmer for 8 minutes. Let cool and set aside.
2. Mix the brussel sprouts in olive oil plus butter. Season with salt and pepper. Cover the pot. Cook low for 4 hours. Drizzle the balsamic vinegar on top of the Brussels sprouts. Sprinkle the Parmesan cheese on top.

Nutrition: Calories 193 Fat 10 g Cholesterol 13.2 mg Carbohydrate 21.9 g Fiber 6.2 g Protein 6.9 g Sugars 11.1 g

190.   Mediterranean Zucchini & Eggplant

Preparation Time: 15 minutes
Cooking Time: 3 hours
Servings: 4

Ingredients:
- 1 tablespoon olive oil
- 1 onion, diced
- 4 cloves garlic, minced
- 1 red bell pepper, chopped
- 4 tomatoes, diced
- 1 zucchini, chopped
- 1 lb. eggplant, sliced into cubes
- Salt and pepper to taste
- 2 teaspoons dried basil
- 4 oz. feta cheese

Directions:
1. Coat your slow cooker with olive oil. Mix all the fixing except cheese in the pot. Cook on high

within 3 hours. Sprinkle feta cheese on top and serve.

Nutrition: Calories 341 Fat 12 g Cholesterol 25 mg Carbohydrate 51 g Fiber 11 g Protein 13 g Sugars 13 g

191.   Roasted Baby Carrots

Preparation Time: 15 minutes
Cooking Time: 6 hours
Servings: 6

Ingredients:
- 2 lb. baby carrots
- ¼ cup apricot preserve
- 6 tablespoons butter
- 2 tablespoons honey
- 1 tablespoon sugar
- 1 teaspoon balsamic vinegar
- 1 teaspoon garlic powder
- Salt and pepper to taste
- ¼ teaspoon dried thyme
- ¼ teaspoon ground mustard

Directions:
1. Combine all the fixing in the slow cooker. Mix well. Cover the pot. Cook on low for 6 hours.

Nutrition: Calories 218 Fat 11.8g Cholesterol 31mg Sodium 206mg Carbohydrate 29.3g Fiber 4.5g Sugars 20.9g Protein 1.3g

192.   Artichokes with Garlic & Cream Sauce

Preparation Time: 15 minutes
Cooking Time: 8 hours
Servings: 6

Ingredients:
- Cooking spray
- 30 oz. canned diced tomatoes
- 6 cloves garlic, crushed and minced
- 28 oz. canned artichoke hearts, rinsed, drained, and sliced into quarters
- ½ cup whipping cream
- 1 teaspoon dried basil
- ½ teaspoon dried oregano
- Feta cheese

Directions:

1. Spray the slow cooker with oil. Add the tomatoes with juice, garlic, and artichoke hearts. Season with the basil and oregano. Mix well. Cover the pot. Cook on low for 8 hours. Stir in the cream. Let sit for 5 minutes. Top with the crumbled cheese.

Nutrition: Calories 403 Fat 5 g Cholesterol 27 mg Carbohydrate 38 g Fiber 5 g Protein 13 g Sugars 17 g

193. Mediterranean Kale & White Kidney Beans

Preparation Time: 30 minutes
Cooking Time: 3 hours
Servings: 6

Ingredients:

- 1 onion, chopped
- 4 cloves garlic, crushed
- ¼ cup celery, chopped
- 2 carrots, sliced
- 1 cup farro, rinsed and drained
- 14 oz. canned roasted tomatoes
- 4 cups low-sodium vegetable broth
- ½ teaspoon red pepper, crushed
- Salt to taste
- 3 tablespoons freshly squeezed lemon juice
- 15-ounce white kidney beans, drained
- 4 cup kale
- ½ cup feta cheese, crumbled
- Fresh parsley, chopped

Directions:

1. Put the onion, garlic, celery, carrots, farro, tomatoes, broth, red pepper, and salt in your slow cooker. Seal the pot. Cook on high for 2 hours. Stir in the lemon juice, beans, and kale. Cover and cook for 1 more hour. Sprinkle the cheese and parsley before serving.

Nutrition: Calories 274 Fat 9 g Cholesterol 11 mg Carbohydrate 46 g Fiber 9 g Protein 14 g Sugars 6 g

194. Creamed Corn

Preparation Time: 10 minutes
Cooking Time: 4 hours
Servings: 12

Ingredients:

- 16 oz. frozen corn kernels
- 8 oz. cream cheese
- ½ cup butter
- ½ cup milk
- 1 tablespoon white sugar
- Salt and pepper to taste

Directions:

1. Put all the listed fixing in the slow cooker. Stir well. Cook on high for 4 hours.

Nutrition: Calories 192 Fat 15 g Cholesterol 42 mg Carbohydrate 13.7 g Fiber 1.3 g Protein 3.4 g Sugars 3 g

195. Spicy Beans & Veggies

Preparation Time: 20 minutes
Cooking Time: 8 hours
Servings: 6

Ingredients:

- 15 ounces canned northern beans, drained
- 15 oz. canned red beans, rinsed and drained
- 5 teaspoons garlic, minced
- 1 onion, chopped
- 1 cup, sliced thinly
- ½ cup celery, sliced thinly
- 2 cups green beans, trimmed and sliced
- 2 red chili peppers, chopped
- 2 bay leaves
- Salt and pepper to taste

Directions:

1. Mix all the fixing listed above in the slow cooker. Set it on low. Seal and cook for 8 hours. Discard the bay leaves before serving.

Nutrition: Calories 264 Fat 0.9g Carbohydrate 49g Sugars 3g Protein 17.2g Potassium 1111mg

196. Eggplant Salad

Preparation Time: 10 minutes
Cooking Time: 8 hours
Servings: 4

Ingredients:

- 1 onion, sliced
- 1 green bell pepper, sliced
- 1 red bell pepper, sliced
- 24 oz. canned tomatoes
- 1 eggplant, sliced
- 2 teaspoons cumin
- 1 tablespoon smoked paprika
- 1 tablespoon lemon juice
- Salt and pepper to taste

Directions:

1. Add all the fixings to the slow cooker. Mix well. Cook on low within 8 hours.

Nutrition: Calories 90 Fat 1.1g Sodium 16mg Carbohydrate 19.7g Fiber 7.9g Sugars 10.9g Protein 3.7g
Potassium 826mg

197.   Turkish Stuffed Eggplant

Preparation time: 15 minutes
Cooking time: 4 hours
Servings: 6

Ingredients:
- ½ cup extra-virgin olive oil
- 3 small eggplants
- 1 teaspoon of sea salt
- ½ teaspoon black pepper
- 1 large yellow onion, finely chopped
- 4 garlic cloves, minced
- one 15-ounce can dice tomatoes, with the juice
- ¼ cup finely chopped fresh flat-leaf parsley
- six 8-inch round pita bread, quartered and toasted
- 1 cup plain Greek-style yogurt

Directions:
1. Pour ¼ cup of the olive oil into the slow cooker, and generously coat the interior of the crock. Cut each eggplant in half lengthwise. You can leave the stem on. Score the cut side of each half every ¼ inch.
2. Arrange the eggplant halves, skin-side down, in the slow cooker. Sprinkle with 1 teaspoon salt and ½ teaspoon pepper. In a large skillet, heat the remaining ¼ cup olive oil over medium-high heat. Sauté the onion and garlic for 3 minutes, or until the onion begins to soften.
3. Add the tomatoes and parsley to the skillet. Season with salt and pepper. Sauté for another 5 minutes, until the liquid has almost evaporated. Using a large spoon, spoon the tomato mixture over the eggplants, covering each half with some of the mixtures.
4. Cover and cook on high within 2 hours or on low for 4 hours. Uncover the slow cooker, and let the eggplant rest for 10 minutes. Then transfer the eggplant to a serving dish. If there is any juice in the bottom of the cooker, spoon it over the eggplant. Serve hot with toasted pita wedges and yogurt on the side.

Nutrition: Calories: 56 Carbs: 10g Fat: 2g Protein: 2g

198.   Eggplant Parmigiana

Preparation time: 15 minutes
Cooking time: 5 hours
Servings: 6

Ingredients:
- 4 mediums to large eggplants, peeled
- sea salt for sweating eggplants, plus 1 teaspoon 2 eggs, lightly beaten
- 1/3 cup vegetable stock
- 3 tablespoons all-purpose flour
- olive oil for frying (about ½ cup)
- 1/3 cup seasoned bread crumbs
- ½ cup grated parmesan cheese, preferably Parmigiano-Reggiano
- 1 tablespoon extra-virgin olive oil
- 1 yellow onion, chopped
- 1 28-ounce can crush tomatoes, with the juice
- 1 6-ounce can tomato paste
- 4 tablespoons chopped fresh parsley
- 2 cloves garlic, minced
- 1 teaspoon dried oregano
- 1 teaspoon of sea salt
- ¼ teaspoon black pepper
- ½ cup white wine
- 16 ounces mozzarella cheese, sliced

Directions:
1. To prepare the eggplant, first, sweat it. Cut the eggplant into ½-inch slices. Put in a large bowl in layers, flavoring each layer with salt. Let it set within 30 minutes to drain excess moisture.
2. Mix the eggs with the stock and flour until smooth in a medium shallow bowl. Soak the eggplant slices in the batter.
3. Warm-up 1 tablespoon of the olive oil for frying in a skillet. Sauté the eggplant in hot olive oil within. Put aside the eggplant on a paper towel-lined plate. Mix the seasoned bread crumbs with the Parmesan cheese in a small bowl. Set aside.
4. Warm-up extra-virgin olive oil in a large skillet over medium heat. Put the onion, then sauté within 3 minutes until the onion begins to soften. Add the crushed tomatoes, tomato paste, parsley, garlic, oregano, 1 teaspoon sea salt, ¼ teaspoon black pepper, and the white wine.
5. Put the fixing in even layers in your slow cooker, in this order: 1/4 of the eggplant slices, 1/4 of the bread crumbs, 1/4 of the tomato mixture, and 1/4 of the mozzarella cheese.
6. Repeat process making three more layers of the eggplant, bread crumbs, tomato mixture, and mozzarella. Cover and cook on low within 4 to 5 hours. Serve hot.

Nutrition: Calories: 270 Carbs: 26g Fat: 15g Protein: 8g

199.   Ratatouille

Preparation time: 15 minutes
Cooking time: 9 hours
Servings: 6
Ingredients:

- 2 large yellow onions, sliced
- 1 large eggplant, unpeeled, sliced
- 4 small zucchinis, sliced
- 2 garlic cloves, minced
- 2 green bell peppers, strips
- 6 large tomatoes, cut into ½-inch wedges
- 1 teaspoon dried basil
- 2 teaspoons sea salt
- ¼ teaspoon black pepper
- 2 tablespoons chopped fresh flat-leaf parsley
- ¼ cup olive oil

Directions:

1. Layer one-half of each of the vegetables in the slow cooker in the following order: onion, eggplant, zucchini, garlic, bell peppers, and tomatoes. Repeat with the other one-half of the vegetables.
2. Sprinkle with the basil, salt, pepper, and parsley. Drizzle the olive oil over the top. Cover and cook on low within 7 to 9 hours. Serve hot.

Nutrition: Calories: 189 Carbs: 15g Fat: 12g Protein: 3g

200.   Slow Cooker Caponata

Preparation time: 15 minutes
Cooking time: 5 hours & 30 minutes
Servings: 8
Ingredients:

- 1-pound plum tomatoes, chopped
- 1 eggplant, not peeled, cut into ½-inch pieces
- 2 medium zucchinis, cut into ½-inch pieces
- 1 large yellow onion, finely chopped
- 3 stalks celery, sliced
- ½ cup chopped fresh parsley
- 2 tablespoons red wine vinegar
- 1 tablespoon brown sugar
- ¼ cup raisins
- ¼ cup (4 ounces) tomato paste
- 1 teaspoon of sea salt
- ¼ teaspoon black pepper
- ¼ cup pine nuts
- 2 tablespoons capers, drained
- 3 tablespoons oil-cured black olives (optional)

Directions:

1. Combine the tomatoes, eggplant, zucchini, onion, celery, and parsley in the slow cooker. Add the vinegar, brown sugar, raisins, and tomato paste. Sprinkle with salt and pepper.
2. Cover and cook on low within 5½ hours, or until thoroughly cooked. Stir in the pine nuts and capers and olives (if using). Serve hot.

Nutrition: Calories: 68 Carbs: 6g Fat: 4g Protein: 1g

201.   Barley-Stuffed Cabbage Rolls with Pine Nuts and Currants

Preparation time: 15 minutes
Cooking time: hours
Servings: 4
Ingredients:

- 1 large head green cabbage, cored
- 1 tablespoon olive oil
- 1 large yellow onion, chopped
- 3 cups cooked pearl barley
- 3 ounces feta cheese, crumbled
- ½ cup dried currants
- 2 tablespoons pine nuts, toasted
- 2 tablespoons chopped fresh flat-leaf parsley
- ½ teaspoon of sea salt
- ½ teaspoon black pepper
- ½ cup apple juice
- 1 tablespoon apple cider vinegar
- 1 15-ounce can crush tomatoes, with the juice

Directions:

1. Steam the cabbage head in a large pot over boiling water for 8 minutes. Remove to a cutting board and let cool slightly. Remove 16 leaves from the cabbage head. Slice off the raised portion of each cabbage leaf (do not cut out the vein).
2. Heat the oil in a large nonstick lidded skillet over medium heat. Add the onion, cover, and cook 6 minutes or until tender. Remove to a large bowl. Stir the barley, feta cheese, currants, pine nuts, and parsley into the onion mixture. Flavor with ¼ teaspoon of the salt and ¼ teaspoon of the pepper.
3. Place cabbage leaves on a work surface. On 1 cabbage leaf, spoon about 1/3 cup of the barley mixture into the center. Fold in the edges of the leaf over the barley mixture and roll the cabbage leaf up. Repeat for the remaining 15 cabbage leaves and filling. Arrange the cabbage rolls in the slow cooker.
4. Combine the remaining ¼ teaspoon salt, ¼ teaspoon pepper, the apple juice, apple cider vinegar, and tomatoes. Pour the apple juice mixture evenly over the cabbage rolls. Cover and cook on high 2 hours or low for 6 to 8 hours. Serve hot.

Nutrition: Calories: 402 Carbs: 70g Fat: 11g Protein: 11g

202.   Balsamic Collard Greens

Preparation time: 15 minutes
Cooking time: 4 hours
Servings: 5

Ingredients:

- 3 bacon slices
- 1 cup chopped sweet onion
- 1-pound fresh collard greens, rinsed, stemmed, and chopped
- ¼ teaspoon of sea salt
- 2 garlic cloves, minced
- 1 bay leaf
- 2 cups vegetable or chicken stock
- 3 tablespoons balsamic vinegar
- 1 tablespoon honey

Directions:

1. Cook or brown the bacon in a medium skillet on medium heat until crisp, about 6 minutes. Put the bacon on a paper towel-lined plate to cool. Crumble the bacon. Add the onion to bacon drippings and cook for 5 minutes, or until tender. Add the collard greens and cook 2 to 3 minutes or until the greens begin to wilt, stirring occasionally.
2. Place the collard greens, salt, garlic, bay leaf, and stock in the slow cooker. Cover and cook on low within 3½ to 4 hours. Combine the balsamic vinegar and honey in a small bowl. Stir the vinegar mixture into the collard greens just before serving. Serve hot, sprinkled with the crumbled bacon.

Nutrition: Calories: 82 Carbs: 0g Fat: 0g Protein: 5g

203.   Glazed Brussels Sprouts with Pine Nuts

Preparation time: 15 minutes
Cooking time: 3 hours
Servings: 6

Ingredients:

- balsamic glaze
- 1 cup balsamic vinegar
- ¼ cup honey
- 2 pounds brussels sprouts, trimmed and halved
- 2 cups vegetable or chicken stock
- 1 teaspoon sea salt & black pepper
- 2 tablespoons extra-virgin olive oil
- ¼ cup pine nuts, toasted
- ¼ cup grated parmesan cheese

Directions:

1. Mix the balsamic vinegar plus honey in a small saucepan over medium-high heat. Stir constantly until the sugar has dissolved. Boil, then adjust the

heat to low and simmer until the glaze is reduced by half, about 20 minutes. The glaze is finished when it will coat the back of a spoon. Set aside.

2. Combine the Brussels sprouts, stock, and ½ teaspoon salt in the slow cooker. Cover and cook on high within 2 to 3 hours, or until the Brussels sprouts are tender.
3. Drain the Brussels sprouts and transfer to a serving dish. Season with salt and pepper. Drizzle with 2 tablespoons or more of the balsamic glaze and the olive oil, then sprinkle with the pine nuts and Parmesan. Serve hot.

Nutrition: Calories: 105 Carbs: 4g Fat: 11g Protein: 2g

204.   Balsamic Root Vegetables

Preparation time: 15 minutes
Cooking time: 5 hours
Servings: 8

Ingredients:

- nonstick cooking oil spray
- 1-pound parsnips, peeled and cut into 1½-inch cubes
- 1-pound carrots, peeled and cut into 1½-inch pieces
- 2 large red onions, coarsely chopped
- ¾ cup dried apricots or figs
- 1½ pounds sweet potatoes, 1½-inch cubes
- 1 tablespoon light brown sugar
- 3 tbsp. olive oil
- 2 tbsp. balsamic vinegar
- 1 tsp sea salt
- ½ teaspoon black pepper
- 1/3 cup chopped fresh flat-leaf parsley

Directions:

1. Coat the interior of the slow cooker crock with nonstick cooking oil spray. Add the parsnips, carrots, onions, and apricots in the prepared slow cooker crock, and layer the sweet potatoes over the top.
2. Whisk the brown sugar, olive oil, balsamic vinegar, salt, and pepper in a small bowl. Pour over vegetable mixture, but do not stir. Cover and cook on high for 4 to 5 hours, or until the vegetables are tender. Toss with parsley just before serving hot.

Nutrition: Calories: 70 Carbs: 13g Fat: 2g Protein: 1g

206. Sweet Potato Gratin

Preparation time: 15 minutes
Cooking time: 4 hours
Servings: 12

Ingredients:

- 1 tablespoon butter, at room temperature
- 1 large sweet onion, thinly sliced
- 2 pounds sweet potatoes, thinly sliced
- 1 tablespoon all-purpose flour
- 1 teaspoon chopped fresh thyme
- ½ teaspoon of sea salt
- ½ teaspoon black pepper
- 2 ounces grated fresh parmesan cheese
- nonstick cooking oil spray
- ½ cup vegetable stock

Directions:

1. Dissolve the butter in a medium nonstick skillet on medium heat. Add the onion and sauté 5 minutes, or until lightly browned. Remove to a large bowl. Add the sweet potatoes, flour, thyme, salt, pepper, and one-half of the grated Parmesan cheese in the large bowl. Toss gently to coat the sweet potato slices with the flour mixture.
2. Coat the slow cooker with cooking oil spray. Transfer the sweet potato mixture to the slow cooker. Pour the stock over the mixture. Sprinkle with the remaining Parmesan. Cover and cook on low within 4 hours or until the potatoes are tender. Serve hot.

Nutrition: Calories: 118 Carbs: 26g Fat: 2g Protein: 1g

207. Orange-Glazed Carrots

Preparation time: 15 minutes
Cooking time: 6 hours
Servings: 8

Ingredients:

- 3 pounds carrots, peeled and cut into ¼-inch slices
- 1½ cups water, plus extra hot water as needed
- 1 tablespoon granulated sugar
- 1 teaspoon of sea salt
- ½ cup orange marmalade
- 2 tablespoons unsalted butter, softened
- 1½ teaspoons fresh sage, minced black pepper (optional)

Directions:

1. Combine the carrots, 1½ cups water, sugar, and 1 teaspoon salt in the slow cooker. Cover and cook on low within 4 to 6 hours.
2. Drain the carrots, and then return to the slow cooker. Stir in the marmalade, butter, and sage.

Season with additional salt and some pepper, if needed. Serve hot.

Nutrition: Calories: 124 Carbs: 30g Fat: 0g Protein: 2g

208. Lemon-Rosemary Beets

Preparation time: 15 minutes
Cooking time: 8 hours
Servings: 7

Ingredients:

- 2 pounds beets, slice into wedges
- 2 tablespoons fresh lemon juice
- 2 tablespoons extra-virgin olive oil
- 2 tbsp. honey
- 1 tablespoon apple cider vinegar
- ¾ teaspoon sea salt
- ½ teaspoon black pepper
- 2 sprigs fresh rosemary
- ½ teaspoon lemon zest

Directions:

1. Place the beets in the slow cooker. Whisk the lemon juice, extra-virgin olive oil, honey, apple cider vinegar, salt, and pepper in a small bowl. Pour over the beets.
2. Add the sprigs of rosemary to the slow cooker. Cover and cook on low within 8 hours, or until the beets are tender. Remove and discard the rosemary sprigs. Stir in the lemon zest. Serve hot.

Nutrition: Calories: 112 Carbs: 18g Fat: 4g Protein: 2g

209. Root Vegetable Tagine

Preparation time: 15 minutes
Cooking time: 9 hours
Servings: 8
Ingredients:
- 1-pound parsnips, peeled and chopped into bite-size pieces
- 1-pound turnips, peeled and chopped into bite-size pieces
- 2 medium yellow onions, chopped into bite-size pieces
- 1-pound carrots, peeled and chopped into bite-size pieces
- 6 dried apricots, chopped
- 6 figs, chopped
- 1 teaspoon ground turmeric
- 1 teaspoon ground cumin
- ½ teaspoon ground ginger
- ½ teaspoon ground cinnamon
- ¼ teaspoon cayenne pepper
- 1 tablespoon dried parsley
- 1 tablespoon dried cilantro (or 2 tablespoons chopped fresh cilantro)
- 1¾ cups vegetable stock

Directions:
1. Combine the parsnips, turnips, onions, carrots, apricots, and figs in the slow cooker. Sprinkle with turmeric, cumin, ginger, cinnamon, cayenne pepper, parsley, and cilantro. Pour in the vegetable stock. Cover and cook within 9 hours on low. Serve hot.

Nutrition: Calories: 131 Carbs: 31g Fat: 1g Protein: 3g

210. Zucchini Casserole

Preparation time: 15 minutes
Cooking time: hours
Servings: 4
Ingredients:
- 1 medium red onion, sliced
- 1 green bell pepper, thin strips
- 4 medium zucchinis, sliced
- one 15-ounce can dice tomatoes, with the juice
- 1 teaspoon of sea salt
- ½ teaspoon black pepper
- ½ teaspoon basil
- 1 tablespoon extra-virgin olive oil
- ¼ cup grated parmesan cheese

Directions:
1. Combine the onion slices, bell pepper strips, zucchini slices, and tomatoes in the slow cooker. Sprinkle with the salt, pepper, and basil.

2. Cover and cook on low within 3 hours. Drizzle the olive oil over the casserole and sprinkle with the Parmesan. Cover and cook on low within for 1½ hours more. Serve hot.

Nutrition: Calories: 219 Carbs: 3g Fat: 16g Protein: 10g

211. Savory Butternut Squash and Apples

Preparation time: 15 minutes
Cooking time: 4 hours
Servings: 10

Ingredients:
- one 3-pound butternut squash, cubed
- 4 cooking apples, peeled, cored, and chopped
- ¾ cup dried currants
- ½ sweet yellow onion such as Vidalia, sliced thin
- 1 tablespoon ground cinnamon
- 1½ teaspoons ground nutmeg

Directions:
1. Combine the squash, apples, currants, and onion in the slow cooker. Sprinkle with the cinnamon and nutmeg. Cook on high within 4 hours, or until the squash is tender and cooked through. Stir while cooking, then serve.

Nutrition: Calories: 300 Carbs: 129g Fat: 2g Protein: 6g

212. Stuffed Acorn Squash

Preparation time: 15 minutes
Cooking time: 6 hours
Servings: 4
Ingredients:
- 1 acorn squash
- 1 tablespoon honey
- 1 tablespoon olive oil (not extra-virgin)
- ¼ cup chopped pecans or walnuts
- ¼ cup chopped dried cranberries
- sea salt

Directions:
1. Cut the squash in half. Discard the seeds and pulp from the middle. Cut the halves in half again to make it into quarters.
2. Place the squash quarters cut-side up in the slow cooker. Combine the honey, olive oil, pecans, and cranberries in a small bowl.
3. Spoon the pecan mixture into the center of each squash quarter. Season the squash with salt. Cook on low within 5 to 6 hours, or until the squash is tender. Serve hot.

Nutrition: Calories: 387 Carbs: 42g Fat: 19g Protein: 12g

213. Baby - Spinach Soup with Nutmeg

Preparation time: 15 minutes
Cooking time: 4 hours
Servings: 4

Ingredients:
- 2 tbsp. of olive oil
- 2 spring onions, sliced
- 2 garlic cloves, sliced
- 4 cups of water
- 1 lb. of baby spinach
- Nutmeg, grated
- 1/4 cup lemon juice
- 4 tbsp. cream (optional)
- Salt
- ground black pepper

Directions:
1. Warm-up oil over medium heat in a large saucepan and sauté onion for 4-5 minutes until soft. Put the onion plus garlic and sauté stirring for another 2 minutes.
2. Add the spinach and stir well; sauté for 2-3 minutes. Transfer the mixture to your Slow Cooker, pour water, lemon juice, and season salt and pepper to taste.
3. Cook on HIGH within 3-4 hours, stirring occasionally. Remove from heat and transfer soup in a blender and blend until smooth. Sprinkle with grated nutmeg. Taste and adjust the lemon juice and salt and pepper. Serve with cream (optional).

Nutrition: Calories: 272 Carbs: 15g Fat: 20g Protein: 4g

214. Basilico Broccoli Soup

Preparation time: 15 minutes
Cooking time: 4 hours
Servings: 6

Ingredients:
- 2 tbsp. olive oil
- 2 green onions finely chopped
- 2 cloves garlic, chopped
- 4 lbs. of broccoli, stems peeled and cut into chunks
- 2 small carrots shredded
- 2 tbsp. fresh basil finely chopped
- 1 tsp fresh ginger grated (inner part)

- 1 cup of water
- 2 cups of bone broth (preferably homemade)
- salt and ground black pepper to taste

Directions:
1. Place all the fixing in your Slow Cooker and stir well. Cook on LOW within 4 hours. Taste and adjust salt and pepper. Serve.

Nutrition: Calories: 270 Carbs: 15g Fat: 17g Protein: 16g

215. Light Sour Artichokes

Preparation time: 15 minutes
Cooking time: 4 hours
Servings: 4

Ingredients:
- 4 large artichoke hearts cleaned
- 2 tbsp. lard
- 1/3 cup lemon juice freshly squeezed
- Water
- Salt and ground black pepper to taste
- fresh thyme finely chopped

Directions:
1. Wash and clean artichokes. With the knife, trim the very bottom of the stem. Grease your Slow Cooker with lard and add artichokes, lemon juice, and season with salt and ground pepper.
2. Pour water enough to cover 3 of the artichokes. Cover the lid and cook on HIGH for 3-4 hours. Sprinkle with fresh thyme and serve.

Nutrition: Calories: 124 Carbs: 14g Fat: 4g Protein: 10g

216. Cheesy Broccoli Soup

Preparation time: 15 minutes
Cooking time: 4 hours
Servings: 5

Ingredients:
- 1 of broccoli, cut into medium-size pieces
- 2 of green onions finely chopped
- 2 cloves of garlic, chopped
- 2 cups bone broth (preferably homemade)
- 2 cups of water
- 1/4 cup butter melted
- 1 1/2 cups grated cheese
- salt and ground black pepper to taste

Directions:

1. Add broccoli, green onions, garlic, bone broth, and water in your Slow Cooker. Cover the lid and cook on LOW within 4 hours.
2. Transfer the soup to your high-fast blender, and add melted butter and shredded cheese. Blend until all ingredients combine well, smooth and creamy. Adjust the salt and pepper and serve.

Nutrition: Calories: 140 Carbs: 13g Fat: 5g Protein: 10g

217. Creamish Chicken Soup with Broccoli

Preparation time: 15 minutes
Cooking time: 5 hours
Servings: 6

Ingredients:

- 1 tbsp. of chicken fat melted
- 1 lb. of chicken breasts boneless skinless, cut into cubes
- Salt
- ground black pepper
- 4 cups of bone broth
- 1 green onion, finely chopped
- 4 tbsp. of almond flour
- 1 cup of heavy cream
- 3/4 cup of grated Parmesan
- 1 1/2 cups of shredded Cheddar
- 1 large head of broccoli, small florets

Directions:

1. Flavor the chicken breasts with salt plus pepper. Pour the chicken fat in your Slow Cooker and add the chicken cubes. Pour the bone broth and green onions. Cover and cook on LOW within 5 hours.
2. Combine the cooking broth, almond flour, cream, Parmesan, and Cheddar. Add broccoli flowerets in a Slow Cooker and pour the broth mixture. Cover and cook on HIGH for 30 to 45 minutes. Serve hot.

Nutrition: Calories: 178 Carbs: 21g Fat: 4g Protein: 15g

218. Duck Breast Soup

Preparation time: 15 minutes
Cooking time: 8 hours & 35 minutes
Servings: 6

Ingredients:

- 1 tbsp. of chicken fat
- 1 lb. of duck breasts boneless cut into pieces
- 1 carrot sliced
- 1 bell pepper (chopped)
- 2 spring onions sliced
- 1/2 lb. of fresh mushrooms
- 2 bay leaf
- salt and ground black pepper to taste
- 1 tsp of paprika flakes
- 3 cups of bone broth or water
- 2 large eggs
- 3 tbsp. of sour cream
- 1/2 cup of parsley, chopped

Directions:

1. Add the chicken fat to your Slow Cooker. Flavor the duck meat with salt plus pepper, and place in Slow Cooker. Add carrots, pepper, spring onions, mushrooms, bay leaves, and paprika flakes; season with the salt and pepper and stir well.
2. Pour the bone broth and cover. Cook on LOW heat for 8 hours. Whisk the eggs with sour cream and a pinch of salt and pepper. Pour the mixture into a Slow Cooker. Sprinkle with chopped parsley and stir well. Cook on LOW again within 30 to 45 minutes. Serve hot.

Nutrition: Calories: 277 Carbs: 23g Fat: 16g Protein: 10g

219. Green Garden Soup

Preparation time: 15 minutes
Cooking time: 5 hours
Servings: 6

Ingredients:

- 1 lb. of fresh spinach, rinsed and chopped
- 2 tbsp. of olive oil
- 1 large zucchini, sliced
- 1 carrot, sliced
- 1 green bell pepper, chopped
- 3 green onions finely chopped
- 1/2 tsp of paprika flakes
- salt to taste
- 4 cups of water

Directions:

1. Rinse and chop spinach. Pour the oil into a Slow Cooker and add spinach; season with a little salt. Add all remaining ingredients and stir. Cover and cook on LOW mode for 4 to 5 hours. Taste and adjust salt to taste. Serve.

Nutrition: Calories: 29 Carbs: 6g Fat: 0g Protein: 2g

220.   Meaty Swiss Chard Stew

Preparation time: 15 minutes
Cooking time: 4 hours
Servings: 4

Ingredients:
- 3 tbsp. of olive oil
- 2 onions finely diced
- Salt and ground pepper to taste
- 3/4 lbs. ground beef
- 3/4 lb. of Swiss chard chopped
- 1/2 cup water
- 1 tsp garlic powder
- 1 tsp ground cumin
- 1 cup of ground or crushed almonds

Directions:
1. Warm the oil in a large frying skillet and sauté onions with a pinch of salt. Add the ground meat and sauté for 2 minutes.
2. Add Swiss chard, water, and spices; stir for one minute and pour the mixture into your Slow Cooker. Sprinkle with almonds, stir, and cover. Cook on HIGH mode for 2 hours or on SLOW within 4 to 5 hours. Taste, adjust seasonings, and serve.

Nutrition: Calories: 238 Carbs: 43g Fat: 1g Protein: 16g

221.   Halibut and Shrimp Bisque

Preparation time: 15 minutes
Cooking time: 9 hours
Servings: 6

Ingredients:
- 1 lb. of halibut fish
- 2 cups of frozen shrimp
- 2 cups of potatoes, small cubes
- 1 onion finely diced
- 1 cup carrot peeled
- 1 celery root
- 6 cloves of garlic
- 2 tsp half-and-half cream
- 3 cups of fish broth
- Salt
- ground black pepper

Directions:
1. Cut the fish and place with remaining ingredients (except the cream and the shrimp) into your Slow Cooker.
2. Cover and cook on LOW within 8-10 hours, or until the potatoes are tender. About 30 minutes before cooking time, stir in Slow Cooker a cup of

cream and the frozen shrimp. Adjust the salt and pepper. Cook on HIGH within 30 minutes. Serve hot.

Nutrition: Calories: 190 Carbs: 13g Fat: 10g Protein: 10g

222.   Healthy Beef Stew

Preparation time: 15 minutes
Cooking time: 8 hours & 45 minutes
Servings: 6

Ingredients:
- 2 tbsp. of olive oil
- 1 1/2 lbs. beef stewing steak cut into large cubes
- 1 large tomato grated
- 2 green chili pepper, finely chopped
- 2 green onions (green parts only, sliced)
- 3 cloves garlic finely chopped
- 1 tbsp. dried oregano
- 2 tsp ground cumin
- 1 tsp of red paprika flakes
- salt and ground red pepper to taste
- 1 cup of water
- 2 to 3 tbsp. breadcrumbs

Directions:
1. Add all the listed fixing in your Slow Cooker (except breadcrumbs) and stir well. Cover lid and cook on LOW heat 8 hours, or until meat is tender. When ready, open the lid and add in the breadcrumbs; stir well. Cover and cook on LOW again within 30 to 45 minutes. Serve immediately.

Nutrition: Calories: 170 Carbs: 0g Fat: 7g Protein: 24g

223.   Slow Cooked Saffron-Marinated Cod Fillets

Preparation time: 15 minutes
Cooking time: 3 hours
Servings: 4

Ingredients:
- 4 Cod fillets without skin
- ½ cup of olive oil
- generous pinch of saffron threads
- 2 splash of apple cider vinegar
- fresh basil finely chopped, to garnish
- 1/2 tsp sea salt
- 1/2 tsp black pepper

Directions:
1. Combine olive oil, saffron threads, salt, pepper, and vinegar in a deep container. Add the fish fillets

and toss well to coat. Sprinkle with a pinch of ground pepper, cover, and leave to marinate in the fridge for about one hour.

2. Place the cod fillet in your Slow Cooker along with the marinade and cover lid. Cover and cook on LOW within 3 hours. Serve hot with chopped basil.

Nutrition: Calories: 140 Carbs: 6g Fat: 5g Protein: 17g

224.   Julienne Vegetable Soup

Preparation time: 15 minutes
Cooking time: 2 hours
Servings: 5

Ingredients:
- 1 carrot cut into julienne strips
- 1 turnip cut into julienne strips
- 7 oz. fresh beans cut into julienne strips
- 2 stalks celery
- 2 cloves garlic (finely minced)
- 1 onion finely sliced
- 2 cups of vegetable broth
- 2 cups of water
- 2 bay leaves
- 1 tsp of fresh thyme finely chopped
- 1 tsp of fresh basil finely chopped
- Salt and ground pepper to taste

Directions:
1. Cut vegetables into lengthwise julienne strips about 1/4 inch thick. Place all vegetables into Slow Cooker. Pour vegetable broth and water; stir and cover. Season with herbs/spices and with salt and pepper. Cover and cook on HIGH within 2 hours. Remove bay leaves, adjust seasonings, and serve.

Nutrition: Calories: 70 Carbs: 10g Fat: 3g Protein: 2g

225.   Spanish Chorizo and Clams Stew

Preparation time: 15 minutes
Cooking time: 40 minutes
Servings: 6

Ingredients:
- 2 tbsp. olive oil
- 2 onions finely diced
- 2 cloves of garlic, mashed
- 12 oz. of Spanish chorizo sausages, finely diced
- 2 potatoes
- 5 lbs. clams, rinsed in cold water
- 2 tbsp. of tomato paste or grated fresh tomato
- 1 cup of beef broth
- 1 1 tsp fresh thyme, chopped
- 2 tsp smoked paprika
- Sea salt
- ground black pepper

Directions:
1. Warm olive oil in a frying skillet and sauté the onion and garlic with a pinch of salt. Add sliced chorizo sausages and tomato paste. Cook on medium heat for 5 minutes. Transfer the mixture and all remaining ingredients into your Slow Cooker and add clams; toss to combine well.
2. Pour the beef broth, fresh thyme, and smoked paprika; stir and cover. Season with the salt and pepper; stir. Cook on HIGH for about 30 to 35 minutes or until clams are tender. Serve hot.

Nutrition: Calories: 166 Carbs: 11g Fat: 6g Protein: 15g

226.   Stringing Nettle and Chicken Soup

Preparation time: 15 minutes
Cooking time: 4 hours & 45 minutes
Servings: 6

Ingredients:
- 1 tbsp. of chicken fat
- 2 chicken breasts, cut into pieces
- 1 carrot sliced
- 2 onions, sliced
- 1 bell pepper, chopped
- 1/2 lb. of nettle cleaned and chopped
- 1 tbsp. of fresh thyme finely chopped
- 3 cups of water
- salt and ground black pepper to taste
- 2 eggs from free-range chicken
- 1 tbsp. of red paprika flakes

Directions:
1. Add chicken fat to your Slow Cooker. Add chicken, carrot, onions, bell pepper, nettle, and fresh thyme. Flavor with the salt and pepper, pour water, and stir well. Cover and cook on LOW for 4 hours. Mix the eggs with salt plus paprika flakes, and pour into Slow Cooker. Cover again, and cook on LOW for an additional 30 to 45 minutes. Serve.

Nutrition: Calories: 121 Carbs: 20g Fat: 3g Protein: 4g

227. Piedmont Fontina Cheese Dip with Truffle Oil Fonduta

Preparation time: 15 minutes
Cooking time: 2 hours
Servings: 4

Ingredients:
- 4 tsp corn flour (cornstarch)
- 2/3 cup milk
- 2 large eggs
- 1½ cups grated Fontina cheese
- 2 tbsp. unsalted (sweet) butter, cut into small flakes
- Salt and freshly ground black pepper
- 6 tbsp. single (light) cream
- 1 tsp truffle oil

Directions:
1. Whisk the corn flour and milk in a small earthenware pot that will fit in the slow cooker. Whisk in the eggs. Stir in the cheese and add the butter and some salt and pepper. Stand the dish in the crockpot with boiling water to come halfway up the side of the dish.
2. Cover and cook on Low within 2 hours or until thick, stirring well every 30 minutes. Remove from the crockpot and beat well, then beat in the cream. Trickle the truffle oil over and serve straight away with ciabatta bread cut into small chunks for dunking.

Nutrition: Calories: 120 Carbs: 0g Fat: 12g Protein: 2g

228. Coarse Pork Terrine with Pistachios

Preparation time: 15 minutes
Cooking time: 10 hours
Servings: 10

Ingredients:
- 12 rashers (slices) of streaky bacon
- 1 Onion, quartered
- 2 Garlic cloves, roughly chopped
- 6 sprigs of fresh parsley
- 1 lb. belly pork, skinned
- 4 oz. unsmoked bacon pieces, trimmed of any rind or gristle
- 12 oz. pig's liver
- 1 tsp dried herbes de Provence
- ¼ tsp ground cloves
- A good pinch of cayenne

- 2 tbsp. brandy
- ¾ cup shelled pistachio nuts
- 1½ tsp salt
- Freshly ground black pepper

Directions:
1. Line a 6-cup terrine or large loaf tin with some bacon rashers, trimming to fit as necessary. Using a food processor or mincer (grinder), process the onion, garlic, parsley, pork, bacon pieces, and liver but not too finely.
2. Stir in the dried herbs, spices, brandy, pistachios, salt, and a good grinding of pepper. Turn into the prepared terrine and level.
3. Top with the remaining bacon. Cover with greaseproof (waxed) paper, then a lid or foil, twisting and folding it under the rim to secure. Stand the terrine in the crockpot with boiling water to come halfway up of the terrine.
4. Cover and cook on Low within 8-10 hours until firm to the touch and the juices are clear. Remove from the crockpot and remove the cover.
5. Top with some clean greaseproof paper and weigh down with heavy weights or cans of food. Leave until cold, then chill. Serve sliced with crusty bread, mustard, and a side salad.

Nutrition: Calories: 97 Carbs: 3g Fat: 5g Protein: 9g

229. Chicken Liver Pâté with Button Mushrooms

Preparation time: 15 minutes
Cooking time: 8 hours
Servings: 10

Ingredients:
- 1 onion, peeled and quartered
- 2 garlic cloves, peeled and roughly chopped
- 1 lb. chicken liver, trimmed
- 2 tbsp. brandy
- ½ tsp dried mixed herbs 2
- 1 cup butter, melted
- 4 tbsp. double (heavy) cream
- 1 egg, beaten
- Salt and freshly ground black pepper
- 6 oz. button mushrooms, sliced
- Mixed salad leaves and lemon wedges to garnish

Directions:
1. Place the onion, garlic, liver, brandy, herbs, three-quarters of butter, cream, and egg in a blender or food processor. Season generously and run the machine to make a smooth paste.

2. Put the remaining melted butter in a saucepan, add the mushrooms, and fry, stirring, for 3 minutes until tender. Turn up the heat, if necessary, to evaporate the liquid. Stir into the pâté mixture.
3. Grease a 6-cup terrine or large loaf tin and line the base with non-stick baking parchment. Spoon the pâté into the tin and level the surface.
4. Cover with greaseproof (waxed) paper, then a lid or foil, twisting and folding under the rim to secure, and place in the slow cooker with enough boiling water to come halfway up the sides of the terrine.
5. Cover and cook on Low within 6-8 hours until firm to the touch. Remove from the crockpot. Remove the lid or foil and re-cover with clean greaseproof paper.
6. Leave to cool, then weigh down with heavy weights or cans of food and chill until firm. Loosen the edge and move it onto a cutting board.
7. Cut into thick slices and arrange on individual plates. Garnish each with a few salad leaves and a lemon wedge and serve with triangles of toast.

Nutrition: Calories: 200 Carbs: 5g Fat: 17g Protein: 3g

230.   Warm Tuscan White Bean Salad

Preparation time: 15 minutes
Cooking time: 8 hours
Servings: 6

Ingredients:
- 11/3 cup dried haricot (navy) beans, soaked in cold water for several hours or overnight
- 4¼ cups boiling water
- 4 slices of Parma (or similar raw) ham, diced 5
- 1/3 cup black olives
- 1 red onion, thinly sliced
- 2 sun-dried tomatoes, chopped
- 1 red (bell) pepper, chopped
- 2 tsp chopped fresh rosemary
- 1 tbsp. chopped fresh basil
- 1 garlic clove, crushed 6
- 4 tbsp. olive oil
- 2 tbsp. white balsamic condiment
- Salt and freshly ground black pepper

Directions:
1. Drain the beans and boil in a saucepan with water. Return to the boil and boil rapidly for 10 minutes. Tip the beans and liquid into the crockpot, cover, and cook on Low for 6-8 hours until the beans are tender.
2. When ready to serve, drain the beans in a colander and tip into a large salad bowl. Put all the rest of

the fixing and season well. Toss well and serve while still warm with ciabatta bread.

Nutrition: Calories: 321 Carbs: 28g Fat: 20g Protein: 9g

231.   Stuffed Garlic Mushrooms with Cream and White Wine

Preparation time: 15 minutes
Cooking time: 7 hours
Servings: 4

Ingredients:
- 1½ cups soft breadcrumbs
- 2 spring onions (scallions), finely chopped
- 2 large garlic cloves, crushed
- 3 tbsp. chopped fresh parsley
- Salt and freshly ground black pepper
- 1 egg, beaten
- 2/3 cup dry white wine 8 tiny knobs of butter
- 2/3 cup double (heavy) cream
- 4 small sprigs of fresh parsley to garnish

Directions:
1. Peel the mushrooms and trim the stalks. Chop the stalks and mix with the breadcrumbs, spring onions, half the garlic, and the parsley. Season well, then mix with the beaten egg.
2. Season the mushroom caps lightly, then press the stuffing mixture onto the gills of each one. Put the wine into the crockpot, add the remaining garlic and a little salt and pepper.
3. Place the mushrooms on top, preferably in a single layer or just overlapping. Top each with a tiny knob of butter.
4. Cover and cook on Low within 5-7 hours until the mushrooms are tender and the stuffing has set. Transfer the mushrooms to small warm plates. Stir the cream into the wine juices, taste, re-season if necessary, and then spoon over. Garnish each plate with a small sprig of parsley and serve with crusty bread.

Nutrition: Calories: 138 Carbs: 5g Fat: 10g Protein: 4g

233. Spanish Tortilla with Piquant Tomato Salsa

Preparation time: 15 minutes
Cooking time: 6 hours
Servings: 4

Ingredients:
For the tortilla:
- 6 tbsp. olive oil
- 2 onions, thinly sliced
- 4 large potatoes, thinly sliced
- 6 eggs
- Salt and freshly ground black pepper

For the salsa:
- 1 tbsp. olive oil
- 1 small onion, chopped
- 1 garlic clove, crushed
- ¼ tsp crushed dried chilies
- 4 beefsteak tomatoes, skinned and chopped
- 4 tbsp. apple juice
- ½ tsp dried oregano
- 2 tbsp. chopped fresh parsley

Directions:
1. To make the tortilla, brush the crockpot with a little of the oil. Warm-up the rest of the oil in a saucepan, add the onions, and fry for 2 minutes, stirring.
2. Add the potatoes and toss well. Cook for within 2 minutes, stirring, then tip the whole lot into the crockpot (keep the pan for making the salsa). Put the mixture as evenly as possible.
3. Cover and cook on Low for 46 hours until the potatoes are tender. Turn the slow cooker to High. Whisk the eggs with salt plus pepper and pour into the pot. Stir well, then cover and cook for 30 minutes until set.
4. Meanwhile, to make the salsa, heat the oil in a saucepan. Put the onion and garlic and cook within 2 minutes until they are softened but not browned. Put all the rest of the fixing except the parsley. Cook rapidly for 5 minutes until pulpy, stirring frequently.
5. Move it to a blender, then blend to a purée. Taste and re-season if necessary, then return to the pan. Reheat when ready to serve. When the tortilla is cooked, remove the crockpot from the base and leave the tortilla cool for 5 minutes. Cut into wedges.
6. Spoon the salsa on to warm plates and place one or two wedges of tortilla on top. Sprinkle with the chopped parsley and serve.

Nutrition: Calories: 140 Carbs: 18g Fat: 3g Protein: 10g

234. Vine Leaves Stuffed with Rice, Herbs, Pine Nuts, and Raisins

Preparation time: 15 minutes
Cooking time: 7 hours
Servings: 24

Ingredients:
- ½ cup pine nuts
- 1/3 cup raisins
- ½ cup short-grain (pudding) rice
- 1 garlic clove, crushed
- 1 small onion, finely chopped
- 1 tsp dried oregano
- 1 tsp dried mint
- 1 tbsp. tomato purée (paste)
- ½ tsp salt Freshly ground black pepper
- ½ tsp ground cinnamon
- 24 vacuum-packed vine leaves, rinsed and dried
- 5 tbsp. olive oil
- Juice of ½ lemon
- 3 cups boiling vegetable stock

Directions:
1. Mix the pine nuts with the raisins, uncooked rice, garlic, onion, herbs, tomato purée, salt, lots of pepper, and cinnamon. Put a filling on each vine leaf, fold in the sides, and roll-up. Pack them tightly into the crockpot.
2. Add the oil and lemon juice, then pour over enough of the boiling stock to cover the vine leaves. Cover and cook on Low within 6-7 hours or until the rice is cooked and most of the liquid has been absorbed.
3. Remove the crockpot from the base and leave the vine leaves to cool in the liquid. Transfer the rolls to a serving platter with a draining spoon and serve at room temperature.

Nutrition: Calories: 170 Carbs: 24g Fat: 2g Protein: 3g

235.   Spanish Mackerel with Roasted Red Peppers

Preparation time: 15 minutes
Cooking time: 2 hours
Servings: 4

Ingredients:

- 1 large onion, halved and thinly sliced
- 2 celery sticks, cut into thin matchsticks
- 2 garlic cloves, finely chopped
- 2 cloves
- 2 bay leaves
- 4 small mackerel, filleted
- 2/3 cup dry white wine
- 6 tablespoon of olive oil, plus extra for drizzling
- 1 tsp light brown sugar
- Salt and freshly ground black pepper
- 4 red (bell) peppers
- 4 small fresh bay leaves, to garnish

Directions:

1. Spread out the onion and celery in the crockpot and sprinkle with the garlic. Add the cloves and bay leaves. Cut the mackerel fillets in halves lengthways and lay them on top, preferably in a single layer or, if not, divided by non-stick baking parchment.
2. Heat the wine, oil, and sugar with a little salt and pepper. Bring to the boil and pour over the mackerel. Cover and cook on Low within 2 hours until the mackerel is tender. Remove the pot, and leave to cool but do not chill.
3. Meanwhile, put the peppers under a preheated grill (broiler) and cook, occasionally turning, for about 15 minutes until the skin has blackened. Put the peppers to rub off the skin in a plastic bag. Discard the stalks and seeds, then cut the flesh into thin strips.
4. Lift the mackerel out of the cooking liquid and discard the cloves and bay leaves. Drain the onion and celery and arrange a small pile on each of four small plates.
5. Top each with two mackerel fillets, then a small pile of red pepper strips. Drizzle with olive oil, garnish each with a small bay leaf, and serve with crusty bread.

Nutrition: Calories: 134 Carbs: 0g Fat: 5g Protein: 20g

236. Apple Olive Cake

Preparation time: 15 minutes
Cooking time: 2 hours
Servings: 4

Ingredients:
- Peeled and chopped Gala apples - 2 large
- Ground cinnamon - ½ teaspoon
- Whole wheat flour - 3 cups
- Orange juice – 2 cups
- Baking powder - 1 teaspoon
- Ground nutmeg - ½ teaspoon
- Sugar - 1 cup
- Baking soda - 1 teaspoon
- Large eggs - 2
- Extra virgin olive oil - 1 cup
- Gold raisins, soaked and drained -2/3 cup
- Confectioner's sugar - for dusting purpose

Directions:
1. In a small bowl, soak the gold raisins in lukewarm water for 15 minutes and drain. Keep aside. Put the chopped apple in a medium bowl and pour orange juice over it. Toss and make sure the apple gets well coated with the orange juice
2. Combine cinnamon, flour, baking powder, nutmeg in a large bowl and keep aside. Add extra virgin olive oil and sugar into the mixture and combine thoroughly.
3. In the large bowl that contains the dry ingredients, make a circular path in the middle part of the flour mixture. Add the olive oil and sugar mixture into this path. Make use of a wooden spoon and stir them well until they blend well with one another. It must be a thick batter.
4. Drain the excess juice from the apples. Add the apples and raisins to the batter and mix it with a spoon to combine. In a six-quart slow cooker, place parchment paper and add the batter over it.
5. Turn the heat setting to low and the timer to two hours or cook until the cake does not have any wet spots over it. Once the cake has cooked well, wait until the cake cools down before cutting them into pieces. Move your cake to a serving dish and sprinkle confectioner's sugar on top.

Nutrition: Calories: 294 Carbohydrate: 47.7g Protein: 5.3g Sugars: 23.5g Fat: 11g Fiber: 4.3g

237. Strawberry Basil Cobbler

Preparation time: 15 minutes
Cooking time: 2 hours & 30 minutes
Servings: 5

Ingredients:
- Divided granulated sugar - 1¼ cups
- Divided whole wheat flour - 2½ cups
- Ground cinnamon - ½ teaspoon
- Baking powder - 2 teaspoons
- Skim milk - ½ cup
- Eggs - 2
- Divided salt - ¼ teaspoon
- Canola oil - 4 tablespoons
- Rolled oats - ¼ cup
- Frozen strawberries - 6 cups
- Vanilla frozen yogurt – 3 cups
- Chopped fresh basil - ¼ cup
- Cooking spray – as required

Directions:
1. Mix the sugar, flour, baking powder, salt, plus cinnamon in a large bowl. Add milk, oil, and eggs into the bowl and combine thoroughly. Coat some olive oil in the bottom of the slow cooker. Transfer and spread the mixed batter evenly into the slow cooker.
2. Take another large bowl and combine flour, salt, and sugar. Add basil and strawberries to the bowl and toss it to coat. Put this batter on the top of the batter in the slow cooker. Top up with the rolled oat mixture. Cook on a high heat within 2½ hours. Serve topped with frozen vanilla yogurt and basil.

Nutrition: Calories: 727 Carbohydrate: 126.8g Sugars: 70.4g Fat: 16.2g Fiber: 5.9g Sodium: 262mg Protein: 19.6g Potassium: 962mg

238.   Pumpkin Pecan Bread Pudding

Preparation time: 15 minutes
Cooking time: 4 hours
Servings: 3

Ingredients:
- Chopped toasted pecans - ½ cup
- Day-old whole-wheat bread cubes - 8 cups
- Eggs - 4
- Cinnamon chips - ½ cup
- Half n half - 1 cup
- Canned pumpkin - 1 cup
- Melted butter - ½ cup
- Brown sugar - ½ cup
- Cinnamon - ½ teaspoon
- Vanilla - 1 teaspoon
- Ground ginger - ¼ teaspoon
- Nutmeg - ½ teaspoon
- Vanilla ice cream - ¼ cup
- Ground cloves – 1/8 teaspoon
- Caramel ice cream topping - ¼ cup

Directions:
1. Grease a 6-quart crockpot and put the bread cubes, cinnamon, and chopped pecans into it. In a medium bowl, whisk pumpkin, eggs, brown sugar, half-n-half, vanilla, melted butter, nutmeg, cinnamon, cloves, ginger, and pour the mixture over the bread cubes. Stir the mix gently.
2. Cover up the slow cooker and cook for 4 hours. It will be well prepared within 4 hours, which you can check by inserting a toothpick, and if it comes clean, it is ready to serve. Before serving, top up with caramel ice cream and vanilla ice cream.

Nutrition: Calories: 289 Carbohydrate: 28g Protein: 6g Sugars: 14g Fat: 17g Fiber: 1g Sodium: 216 mg Potassium: 166mg

239.   Chocolate Fondue

Preparation time: 15 minutes
Cooking time: 2 hours
Servings: 3

Ingredients:
- Chocolate Almonds candy bars - 4½ ounces
- Butter - 1½ tablespoons
- Milk - 3 tablespoons
- Miniature marshmallows - 1½ cup
- Heavy whipping cream - ½ cup

Directions:

1. Grease a 2-quart slow cooker and put chocolate, butter, milk, marshmallows into it. Close the cooker and cook on low heat setting for 1½ hours. Stir the mix every 30 minutes to melt and mix whipping cream gradually. After adding whipping cream, allow it to settle for 2 hours. Use it as a chocolate dip.

Nutrition: Calories: 463 Carbohydrate: 3901g Protein: 5.5g Sugars: 29.4g Fat: 31.8g Fiber: 4.5g Sodium: 138mg Potassium: 30mg

240.   Chocolate Orange Volcano Pudding

Preparation time: 15 minutes
Cooking time: 2 hours
Servings: 6

Ingredients:
- Self-rising flour – ½ pound
- Melted butter - 3½ ounces
- Sifted cocoa - 2¾ ounces
- Caster sugar - 5¼ ounces
- Zest and juice of orange - 1
- Baking powder - 1 teaspoon
- Orange flavored milk chocolate, chopped into chunks - 5¼ ounces
- Milk - 1½ cup
- Salt – a pinch
- Water – 2 cups
- For the Sauce:
- Cocoa – 1 ounce
- Light brown soft sugar - 7½ ounces

Topping:
- Vanilla ice cream - ¼ cup
- Orange wedges – 1 orange
- Cream - ¼ cup

Directions:
1. Grease the slow cooker with butter. Combine the caster sugar, flour, baking powder, and cocoa, pinch of salt, and orange zest in a large mixing bowl thoroughly. Whisk the eggs, orange juice, milk, and buttermilk in a medium bowl. Put it to the dry fixing and combine to form a smooth mixture.
2. Stir in chocolate pieces and then transfer the mixture into the slow cooker. Prepare the sauce by mixing cocoa and sugar in two cups of boiling water. Pour the sauce over the pudding mixture. Cook on a high heat within two hours. Before serving, top the pudding with vanilla ice cream or cream and orange wedges.

Nutrition: Calories: 733 Carbohydrate: 120.8g Protein: 11.8g Sugars: 79.3g Fat: 25.4g Fiber: 8.3g Cholesterol: 48mg Sodium: 259mg Potassium: 607mg

241.   Nutella Fudge

Preparation time: 15 minutes
Cooking time: 1 hour & 30 minutes
Servings: 5

Ingredients:
- Vanilla essence - 1 teaspoon
- Condensed milk – 14 ounces
- 70 percent dark chocolate - 7 0unces
- Nutella - 1 cup
- Chopped toasted hazelnuts - 4 ounces
- Icing sugar - 3 ounces

Directions:
1. In a slow cooker, add vanilla essence, condensed milk, dark chocolate, and Nutella. Cook it for 1½ hours without covering the lid. Make sure to stir the ingredients every ten minutes until they melt completely. Transfer its content into a large-sized mixing bowl
2. Stir in the sieved icing sugar. Take the warm fudge and carefully scrape it flat, and allow it cool. Sprinkle the hazelnuts over the fudge and slightly press them downwards so that they get attached well. Refrigerate this well for 4 hours and then cut them into squares.

Nutrition: Calories: 191 Carbohydrate: 24.7g Protein: 3.2g Sugars: 22.4g Fat: 9.3gFiber: 1.4g Cholesterol: 5mg Sodium: 25mg

242.   Greek Yogurt Chocolate Mousse

Preparation time: 15 minutes
Cooking time: 2 hours
Servings: 4

Ingredients:
- Dark chocolate - 3½ ounces
- Milk - ¾ cup
- Maple syrup - 1 tablespoon
- Greek yogurt - 2 cups
- Vanilla extract - ½ teaspoon

Directions:
1. Pour milk into a glass bowl that can be placed inside the slow cooker. Add the chocolate, either as finely chopped or as a grated one, into the glass bowl. Place the bowl inside the slow cooker. Pour water surrounding the bowl. Cook it within 2 hours on low heat by stirring intermittently.

2. Once the chocolate is combined thoroughly with the milk, turn off the cooker and remove the slow cooker's glass bowl. Put the vanilla extract plus maple syrup in the bowl and stir well. Spoon the Greek yogurt in a large bowl and add the chocolate mixture on top of it. Mix it well before serving. Refrigerate for two hours before serving.

Nutrition: Calories: 170 Carbohydrate: 20.4g Protein: 3.4g Sugars: 17.9g Fat: 8.3g Fiber: 0.8g Sodium: 42mg Potassium: 130mg

243.   Peanut Butter Banana Greek Yogurt Bowl

Preparation time: 15 minutes
Cooking time: 2 hours
Servings: 4

Ingredients:
- Sliced bananas - 2
- Vanilla Greek yogurt - 4 cups
- Flaxseed meal - ¼ cup
- Creamy natural peanut butter - ¼ cup
- Nutmeg - 1 teaspoon

Directions:
1. Divide the yogurt between four different bowls and top it with banana slices. Add peanut butter into a small-sized glass bowl and place it in the slow cooker. Pour water surrounding the glass bowl. Under low heat setting, cook without covering the slow cooker until the peanut butter starts to melt.
2. Once the butter turns to the required thickness, remove the bowl from the slow cooker. Now, scoop one tablespoon of melted peanut butter and serve into the bowl with yogurt and bananas. For each bowl, add about one tablespoon of melted peanut butter. Sprinkle ground nutmeg and flaxseed.

Nutrition: Calories: 187 Carbohydrate: 19g Protein: 6g Sugars: 9g Fat: 10.7g Fiber: 4.5g Sodium: 77mg Potassium: 375mg

244.   Banana Foster

Preparation time: 15 minutes
Cooking time: 2 hours
Servings: 4

Ingredients:
- Bananas – 4
- Butter, melted – 4 tablespoons
- Rum - ¼ cup
- Brown sugar – 1 cup
- Cinnamon, ground - ½ teaspoon
- Vanilla extract – 1 teaspoon
- Coconut, shredded - ¼ cup
- Walnuts, chopped - ¼ cup

Directions:
1. Peel the bananas, slice, and keep ready to use. Place the sliced bananas in the slow cooker in layers. Mix the brown sugar, vanilla, butter, rum, and cinnamon in a medium bowl thoroughly. Pour the mix over the bananas. Cook on low heat for 2 hours. Sprinkle shredded coconut and walnuts on top before 30 of the end processes.

Nutrition: Calories: 539   Carbohydrates: 83.7g
Cholesterol: 31mg Fiber: 4.7g Protein: 3g
Potassium: 567mg Sodium: 101mgSugars: 69g

245.   Rice Pudding

Preparation time: 15 minutes
Cooking time: 2 hours
Servings: 8

Ingredients:
- Glutinous white rice, uncooked – 1 cup
- Evaporated milk – 12 ounces
- Cinnamon stick – 1 ounce
- White sugar – 1 cup
- Nutmeg, ground – 1 teaspoon
- Vanilla extract – 1 teaspoon

Directions:
1. In a 6-quart slow cooker, put all the ingredients. Cover the lid and cook on low heat for 1½ hours. Stir while cooking in progress. Once ready, discard the cinnamon stick and serve.

Nutrition: Calories: 321   Carbohydrates: 56.4g
Cholesterol: 24mg Fiber: 2.6g Protein: 8.2g Sodium: 102mg Potassium: 322mg Sugars: 35g

246.   Bittersweet Cocoa Almond Cake

Preparation time: 15 minutes
Cooking time: 2 hours & 30 minutes
Servings: 8

Ingredients:
- 4 tablespoons (½ stick) unsalted butter, melted and cooled, plus more for the pan
- ½ cup whole almonds (with skins), lightly toasted
- 1¼ cups Dutch-process cocoa
- 1 cup of water
- 1 teaspoon vanilla extract
- ¾ cup of sugar
- 3 large eggs, plus 2 egg whites
- Pinch of salt
- 2 tablespoons sliced almonds (with skins)
- Whipped cream

Directions:
1. Butter a 6-cup soufflé dish. Arrange the bottom of the dish with wax paper, then butter the paper. Place a rack in a large slow cooker. Put the whole almonds in your food processor fitted with the steel blade. Process until finely ground. Remove from the processor.
2. Put the cocoa, water, and vanilla into the processor and process until smooth. Add the 4 tablespoons melted butter and ½ cup of the sugar and mix well for about 30 seconds. While the machine is running, put the whole eggs, one at a time, and process until smooth, about 30 seconds more. Stir in the ground almonds.
3. Whisk the egg whites plus the salt on medium speed until light and fluffy in a large bowl with an electric mixer. Adjust the speed to high and beat in the remaining ¼ cup sugar until soft peaks form about 3 minutes. Mix the cocoa batter into the egg white mixture. Scrape the batter into the prepared dish.
4. Put it on the rack of your slow cooker, then pour hot water about 1 inch. Cook on high within 2½ hours, or until just set. Carefully remove the dish from the cooker. Let cool for 20 minutes.
5. Cover with an inverted bowl and refrigerate for several hours or overnight. Just before serving, sprinkle the cake with the sliced almonds. Slice and serve with whipped cream.

Nutrition: Calories: 276 Carbs: 20g Fat: 19g Protein: 0g

248.   Apricot Almond Cake

Preparation time: 15 minutes
Cooking time: 3 hours
Servings: 8

Ingredients:

- 4 tablespoons (½ stick) unsalted butter, softened, plus more for the pan
- 1 cup whole almond (with skins), toasted
- 1 cup of sugar
- ½ cup all-purpose flour
- ¼ teaspoon baking powder
- 4 large eggs, at room temperature
- 1 teaspoon vanilla extract
- ¼ teaspoon almond extract

Apricot Glaze:

- 1/3 cup apricot jam
- 2 tablespoons sugar
- 2–3 tablespoons sliced almonds (with skins), toasted

Directions:

1. Butter a 7-x-2-inch round cake pan. Put wax paper in the pan and butter the paper. Put a rack in a large slow cooker. Put 2 cups of hot water into the cooker and turn on.
2. Mix the whole almonds and ¼ cup of the sugar in a food processor. Process just until very finely ground, about 1 minute. Put the flour plus baking powder, pulse 2 or 3 times to blend.
3. Whisk the 4 tablespoons butter and the remaining ¾ cup sugar on medium speed until very light and fluffy in a large bowl using an electric mixer. Whisk in the eggs, one at a time, until smooth and well blended. Scrape down the sides of the bowl.
4. Beat in the vanilla and almond extracts. With a rubber spatula, fold in the ground almond mixture. Scrape the batter into the prepared pan. Place the cake pan in the slow cooker. Cook on high within 3 hours. Remove, then let cool for 10 minutes.
5. Make the apricot glaze: Heat the jam and sugar in a small saucepan over medium heat. When the mixture starts to simmer, stir well until melted. Strain the glaze through a fine-mesh sieve into a small bowl, pressing on the solids.
6. Put the glaze over the top of the cake and spread it smooth. Sprinkle the sliced almonds in a border around the top edge of the cake. Let cool before serving.

Nutrition: Calories: 228 Carbs: 7g Fat: 19g Protein: 8g

249.   Walnut Cake with Cinnamon Syrup

Preparation time: 15 minutes
Cooking time: 2 hours & 20 minutes
Servings: 8

Ingredients:

- Unsalted butter for the pan
- 1 cup toasted walnuts
- ½ cup of sugar
- ½ cup all-purpose flour
- 1 teaspoon baking powder
- 1 teaspoon ground cinnamon
- ½ teaspoon grated lemon zest
- Pinch of salt
- 2 large eggs, plus 1 egg yolk
- ½ cup plain Greek-style yogurt
- ¼ cup olive oil

Cinnamon Syrup:

- 1 cup of sugar
- ½ cup of water
- 1 3-inch cinnamon stick
- 1 2-inch strip lemon zest

Directions:

1. Butter a 7-x-2-inch round cake pan or a 6-cup soufflé dish. Arrange the bottom of the pan with wax paper plus butter the paper. Put a rack in a large slow cooker. Pour 2 cups hot water into the cooker, and turn on the cooker.
2. Mix the walnuts and ¼ cup of the sugar in a food processor within 1 minute. Add the flour, baking powder, ground cinnamon, lemon zest, and salt. Pulse 2 or 3 times to blend.
3. In another bowl, whisk the whole eggs, the egg yolk, the remaining ¼ cup sugar, the yogurt, and olive oil. Stir in the dry ingredients. Scrape the batter into the prepared pan. Put the cake pan on the rack in the slow cooker. Cook on high within 2¼ hours. Let it cool.
4. For the cinnamon syrup, mix all the syrup ingredients in a small saucepan. Simmer within 10 minutes, or until slightly thickened. Let cool.
5. Slide the cake onto a serving dish. Remove the cinnamon stick and the lemon zest from the syrup. Pour the syrup over the cake. Let it stand within 1 hour before serving so that the cake can absorb some of the syrup.

Nutrition: Calories: 260 Carbs: 32g Fat: 13g Protein: 3g

251. Sunny Orange Cake with Orange Syrup

Preparation time: 15 minutes
Cooking time: 2 hours & 30 minutes
Servings: 8
Ingredients:
- 4 tablespoons (½ stick) unsalted butter, softened, plus more for the pan
- ½ cup all-purpose flour
- ½ cup fine semolina or farina
- 1 teaspoon baking powder
- ½ cup of sugar
- 2 large eggs, separated
- 1 teaspoon vanilla extract
- ½ teaspoon grated orange zest
- ½ cup whole milk
- Pinch of salt

Orange Syrup:
- ¾ cup of sugar
- ¾ cup of orange juice
- ½ teaspoon grated orange zest
- Fresh orange slices and mint leaves

Directions:
1. Put a rack in a large slow cooker. Butter a round cake pan. Line the bottom of the pan with wax paper and butter the paper. Stir the flour, semolina, and baking powder. Whisk the 4 tablespoons butter and the sugar in a large bowl using an electric mixer on medium speed within 2 minutes.
2. Put the egg yolks, then beat until light, about 3 minutes. Beat in the vanilla and orange zest. Put the flour batter in 3 additions, alternating with the milk and beginning and ending with the flour.
3. Beat the egg whites and the salt in a medium bowl on medium speed until soft peaks form. Fold the egg whites with the semolina mixture. Scrape the mixture into the prepared pan. Place the pan on in the slow cooker. Put the hot water around the cake pan to a depth of 1 inch. Cook on high within 2 to 2½ hours.
4. For the orange syrup, combine the sugar and orange juice in a small saucepan. Simmer the mixture within 5 minutes. Stir in the orange zest. Remove from the heat and let cool.
5. Slowly put the orange syrup on the cake. Let it set within 1 hour so that the cake can absorb some of the syrup. Serve with the orange slices and mint leaves.

Nutrition: Calories: 300 Carbs: 36g Fat: 15g Protein: 7g

252. Two-Berry Clafouti

Preparation time: 15 minutes
Cooking time: 2 hours
Servings: 6

Ingredients:
- 2 cups fresh blueberries
- 1 cup fresh raspberry
- 1 3-ounce package cream cheese, softened
- ½ cup of sugar
- 3 large eggs
- ½ cup milk
- ½ teaspoon grated lemon or orange zest
- ¼ cup all-purpose flour
- Confectioners' sugar for sprinkling

Directions:
1. Oiled the insert of a large slow cooker with nonstick cooking spray. Scatter the berries in the slow cooker. Mix the cream cheese and sugar in a blender. Add the eggs, milk, and zest and blend well. Put the flour and blend within 1 minute. Pour the mixture over the berries.
2. Cook on high within 1½ to 2 hours, or until the clafouti is slightly puffed and the center jiggles slightly when the sides are tapped. Allow cooling to room temperature. Scoop onto serving plates and serve, sprinkled with confectioners' sugar.

Nutrition: Calories: 200 Carbs: 6g Fat: 0g Protein: 0g

253.   Cannoli Cheesecake

Preparation time: 15 minutes
Cooking time: 2 hours & 30 minutes
Servings: 8

Ingredients:
- Unsalted butter for the pan
- 1 15- to 16-ounce container whole-milk ricotta
- 6 ounces cream cheese, softened
- 2/3 cup confectioners' sugar
- ½ teaspoon ground cinnamon
- 1 teaspoon vanilla extract
- 2 large eggs
- ½ cup miniature semisweet chocolate chips
- 2 tablespoons chopped candied orange peel or 1 teaspoon grated orange zest
- ½ cup coarsely chopped unsalted pistachios

Directions:
1. Put a rack in a large slow cooker. Butter a 7-inch pan. Put the pan in the center of an aluminum foil and wrap the foil around the sides so that water cannot enter.
2. Whisk the ricotta and cream cheese with the confectioners' sugar, cinnamon, and vanilla until very smooth, about 5 minutes in a food processor. Add the eggs and process until blended, about 2 minutes.
3. With a spoon, lightly stir in the chocolate chips and candied orange peel. Pour the mixture into the prepared pan. Put hot water around the pan. Cook on high within 2½ hours. Press the pistachios onto the sides of the cake. Cut into wedges and serve.

Nutrition: Calories: 358 Carbs: 36g Fat: 20g Protein: 12g

254.   Chocolate Hazelnut Cheesecake

Preparation time: 15 minutes
Cooking time: hours
Servings: 8

Ingredients:
- 3 tbsp. dissolved unsalted butter, plus more for the pan
- 2/3 cup chocolate wafer, cookie crumbs
- 1 15- to 16-ounce container whole-milk ricotta
- 2/3 cup Nutella or other chocolate hazelnut spread
- ¼ cup of sugar
- 2 large eggs

Directions:
1. Put a rack in a slow cooker. Butter a 7-inch pan. Put the pan in the center of a large sheet of aluminum foil and wrap it around the sides so that water cannot enter. Mix the cookie crumbs, and the 3 tablespoons melted butter in a small bowl. Put the mixture firmly into the base of the prepared pan. Place the pan in the refrigerator.
2. Beat the ricotta and Nutella with the sugar until very smooth, about 2 minutes in a food processor. Put the eggs, one at a time, and process until blended. Pour the mixture into the pan. Put the pan on the rack of your slow cooker. Put hot water to a depth of about 1 inch around the pan. Cook on high within 2½ hours. Cut into wedges and serve.

Nutrition: Calories: 210 Carbs: 22g Fat: 13g Protein: 1g

255.   Coffee Caramel Flan

Preparation time: 15 minutes
Cooking time: 2 hours & 30 minutes
Servings: 8

Ingredients:
- 1 cup of sugar
- ¼ cup of water
- 1 12-ounce can evaporate milk
- 1 14-ounce can sweeten condensed milk
- 2 large eggs, plus 2 egg yolks
- 2 tbsp. espresso powder melted in 1 tablespoon hot water

Directions:
1. Put a rack in your large slow cooker. Mix the sugar plus water in a small saucepan. Cook over medium heat within 5 minutes. Simmer the mixture within 10 minutes.
2. Put the hot syrup into a 6-cup soufflé dish, then let it cool. Whisk the evaporated milk and condensed milk in a medium bowl. Beat in the eggs, yolks, and espresso until blended. Pour the mixture into the soufflé dish.
3. Put the dish on the rack in your slow cooker. Put hot water to a depth of 1 inch around. Cook on high within 2 to 2½ hours. Let it cool, and refrigerate within several hours or overnight. Carefully remove the dish. Cut into wedges and serve.

Nutrition: Calories: 130 Carbs: 25g Fat: 3g Protein: 3g

256.   Coconut Flan

Preparation time: 15 minutes
Cooking time: 3 hours & 30 minutes
Servings: 8

Ingredients:

- ½ cup of sugar
- ¼ cup of water
- 1 12-ounce can evaporate milk
- 1 15-ounce can cream of coconut
- 4 large eggs
- 1 tablespoon brandy or rum or 1 teaspoon vanilla extract

Directions:

1. Put a rack in a large slow cooker. Mix the sugar plus water in a saucepan. Cook on medium heat within 5 minutes. Simmer within 10 minutes, then put the hot syrup into a 6-cup soufflé dish.
2. In a medium bowl, whisk the evaporated milk and cream of coconut. Beat in the eggs and brandy until blended. Pour the mixture into the soufflé dish.
3. Put it on the rack in the slow cooker. Pour hot water of 1 inch around it. Cover and cook on high within 3 to 3½ hours. Carefully remove the dish, then slice into wedges and serve.

Nutrition: Calories: 290 Carbs: 46g Fat: 9g Protein: 7g

257.   Lemon Cheese Flan

Preparation time: 15 minutes
Cooking time: 2 hours & 30 minutes
Servings: 8

Ingredients:

- 1½ cups sugar
- ¼ cup of water
- 1 8-ounce package cream cheese, softened
- 1 12-ounce can evaporate milk
- 3 large eggs
- 1 teaspoon grated lemon zest
- 1 teaspoon vanilla extract

Directions:

1. Put a rack in the slow cooker. Mix one cup of the sugar and the water in a small saucepan. Cook on medium heat within 5 minutes. Simmer within 10 minutes. Put the hot syrup into a 6-cup soufflé dish, let it cool until the caramel is just set.
2. Mix the remaining ½ cup sugar, the cream cheese, evaporated milk, eggs, lemon zest, and vanilla until blended in a large bowl. Pour the mixture into the soufflé dish, then in your slow cooker. Put hot water to a depth of 1 inch around the soufflé dish.
3. Cover and cook on high within 2 to 2½ hours. Remove, then let it cool until chilled in the fridge, several hours or overnight. Serve.

Nutrition: Calories: 359 Carbs: 31g Fat: 24g Protein: 13g

258.   Apple Raisin Soufflé Pudding

Preparation time: 15 minutes
Cooking time: 2 hours
Servings: 8

Ingredients:

- 6 large sweet apples, such as Golden Delicious, peeled and thinly sliced
- 1 cup golden raisins
- ¼ cup of sugar
- 2 tablespoons unsalted butter, melted
- 1 teaspoon grated lemon zest
- 2 tablespoons all-purpose flour
- 2 tablespoons cognac or rum

Topping:

- 8 tablespoons (1 stick) unsalted butter, softened
- ½ cup of sugar
- 3 large eggs, separated
- 1 cup milk
- 2 tablespoons cognac or rum (optional)
- ½ cup all-purpose flour
- Pinch of salt

Directions:

1. Grease the insert of your large slow cooker with nonstick cooking spray. Add the apples, raisins, sugar, butter, lemon zest, flour, and cognac and toss well. Cover and cook on high within 1½ to 2 hours, or until the apples are softened but not quite tender.
2. Make the topping: When the apples are almost ready, beat the butter with the sugar using an electric mixer in a bowl within 3 minutes. Add the egg yolks and blend well. In a small bowl, stir the milk and cognac, if using. Gently stir the milk mixture into the sugar mixture in 3 additions, alternating with the flour in 2 additions.
3. Whisk the egg whites plus salt on medium speed until foamy in a large bowl with clean beaters. Continue beating until soft peaks form. Mix the egg whites into the yolk batter. Stir the apples. Scrape the topping over the apples.
4. Cover and cook on high within 1 hour. Uncover and remove the insert from the cooker. Let cool slightly. Scoop the pudding onto serving plates and serve warm or at room temperature.

Nutrition: Calories: 300 Carbs: 47g Fat: 9g Protein: 9g

259.   Pistachio and Golden Raisin Bread Pudding

Preparation time: 15 minutes
Cooking time: 3 hours

Servings: 8

Ingredients:

- 8 ounces French bread, torn into bite-size pieces and lightly toasted (about 6 cups)
- ½ cup golden raisins
- ½ cup unsalted pistachios
- 6 large eggs
- ½ cup of sugar
- 1 teaspoon ground cinnamon
- ¼ cup honey
- 1 tablespoon grated orange zest
- 3 cups of milk
- 1½ teaspoons vanilla extract

Directions:

1. Oiled the insert of a large slow cooker with nonstick cooking spray. Scatter the bread, raisins, and pistachios in the cooker. Mix the eggs until frothy in a large bowl. Beat in the sugar, cinnamon, honey, and orange zest. Stir in the milk and vanilla.
2. Put the liquid over the bread mixture and stir. Cook on high within 2½ to 3 hours, or until the center is just barely set and slightly puffed. Uncover and remove the insert from the cooker. Let cool slightly. Scoop the pudding into bowls and serve warm.

Nutrition: Calories: 120 Carbs: 27g Fat: 0g Protein: 3g

260. White Chocolate Bread Pudding with Rasp Berried Strawberries

Preparation time: 15 minutes
Cooking time: 2 hours & 30 minutes
Servings: 8

Ingredients:

- 1 cup chopped white chocolate (10 ounces)
- 2 cups milk, heated until hot
- 2/3 cup sugar
- 1 cup heavy cream
- 4 large eggs, beaten
- 2 teaspoons vanilla extract
- 8 ounces brioche or challah bread, cut into 1-inch cubes and lightly toasted (about 6 cups)
- 1-pint strawberries, sliced
- 2–3 tablespoons seedless raspberry jam

Directions:

1. Oiled the insert of a large slow cooker with nonstick cooking spray. Place the white chocolate in a large, heatproof bowl. Add the hot milk and sugar and let stand for 5 minutes. Stir until the white chocolate is melted and the sugar is dissolved.
2. Whisk the cream, eggs, and vanilla and stir the mixture into the white chocolate mixture. Scatter the bread cubes in the slow cooker. Pour the white chocolate mixture over the bread. Cover and cook on high for 1 hour. Adjust the heat to low and cook within 1½ hours, or until the pudding is softly set in the center.
3. Uncover and remove the insert from the cooker. Let cool slightly. Meanwhile, toss the berries with the jam and let stand for 30 minutes, until juicy. Scoop the pudding into bowls. Top with the marinated strawberries and serve.

Nutrition: Calories: 372 Carbs: 31g Fat: 25g Protein: 5g

261. Rice Pudding Brûlée

Preparation time: 15 minutes
Cooking time: 3 hours
Servings: 8

Ingredients:
- 4 cups of milk
- 1 cup heavy cream
- ¾ cup Arborio rice or another short-grain white rice
- 2 2-inch strips of orange zest
- 1 3-inch cinnamon stick
- Pinch of salt
- 2 tablespoons brandy
- ¾ cup of sugar
- Pinch of ground cinnamon

Directions:
1. Oiled the insert of a large slow cooker with nonstick cooking spray. Put the milk and cream into the slow cooker. Stir in the rice, orange zest, cinnamon stick, and salt.
2. Cover and cook on high within 2½ to 3 hours, stirring 2 or 3 times so that the rice doesn't stick to the bottom until the rice is tender. Stir in the brandy and ½ cup of the sugar.
3. Cover and cook for 20 minutes more, or until the sugar dissolves. Remove the cinnamon stick and orange zest. Spread the pudding in a shallow, flameproof baking dish and smooth the top.
4. Put a piece of plastic wrap on the pudding and chill within 2 hours or overnight. Just before serving, position an oven rack about 3 inches from the broiler. Turn the broiler to high. Remove the plastic wrap and place the dish on a baking sheet.
5. Stir the remaining ¼ cup sugar and the ground cinnamon. Put the mixture over the surface of the pudding. Place under the broiler for 2 to 3 minutes, or until the sugar is browned and bubbling. Remove the baking dish and let cool for 5 minutes before serving.

Nutrition: Calories: 70 Carbs: 12g Fat: 2g Protein: 2g

262. Blushing Pomegranate Pears

Preparation time: 15 minutes
Cooking time: 3 hours & 5 minutes
Servings: 8

Ingredients:
- 2/3 cup sugar
- 2 cups pomegranate juice
- 2 3-inch strips of orange zest
- 10 whole black peppercorns
- 8 firm-ripe pears, such as Bosc or Anjou, peeled
- 2 tablespoons chopped unsalted pistachios or sliced almonds

Directions:
1. In a large slow cooker, stir the sugar and juice. Add the orange zest and peppercorns. Put the pears upright in the cooker and put some of the liquid over them. Cook on high within 3 hours, or until the pears are tender when pierced with a knife. Move the pears to a serving dish.
2. Drain the juices through a fine-mesh sieve into a small saucepan. Simmer the juices within 5 minutes. Pour the syrup over the pears. Chill until serving time. Just before serving, sprinkle the pears with the nuts.

Nutrition: Calories: 210 Carbs: 30g Fat: 8g Protein: 4g

263. Tea-Spiced Pears

Preparation time: 15 minutes
Cooking time: 4 hours
Servings: 8

Ingredients:
- 2 Earl Grey tea bags
- 1 cup boiling water
- 1 cup dry white wine
- ¾ cup of sugar
- 1 2-inch strip orange zest
- 4 whole cloves
- 2 whole star anise
- 8 Bosc, Bartlett, or Anjou pears
- Crème fraîche or whipped cream

Directions:
1. Let the tea bags stand in boiling water within 3 minutes. Remove, then pour the tea into a large slow cooker. Add the wine, sugar, orange zest, cloves, and star anise and stir well. Wash the pears and place them standing upright in the slow cooker.
2. Cook on low within 4 hours, or until the pears are tender when pierced with a knife. Remove the pears from the syrup. Strain the syrup over the

pears. Let cool slightly, then cover and refrigerate. Serve chilled with a dollop of crème fraîche.

Nutrition: Calories: 200 Carbs: 51g Fat: 0g Protein: 1g

264.   Honeyed Pears with Goat Cheese and Thyme Pears

Preparation time: 15 minutes
Cooking time: 4 hours
Servings: 8

Ingredients:

- 8 Bosc, Bartlett, or Anjou pears
- 1 lemon
- ½ cup of water
- ½ cup honey
- 4 ounces fresh goat cheese, sliced
- Fresh thyme sprigs

Directions:

1. Wash the pears and place them standing upright in a large slow cooker. Peel off a 2-inch strip of lemon zest. Squeeze the lemon to get 2 tablespoons juice. In a measuring cup, combine the water, honey, and lemon juice and stir well. Pour the liquid over the pears. Add the zest. Cover and cook on low within 4 hours or on high for 2 hours.
2. Carefully remove the pears from the cooker and pour the juices overall. Cover and chill until serving time. Place a pear on each serving plate. Add a slice or two of goat cheese and garnish with a few thyme sprigs.

Nutrition: Calories: 165 Carbs: 4g Fat: 13g Protein: 9g

265.   Lemon Pots de Crème Smooth

Preparation time: 15 minutes
Cooking time: 2 hours
Servings: 4

Ingredients:

- 1/3 cup fresh lemon juice
- ½ teaspoon grated lemon zest
- ½ cup of sugar
- 4 large egg yolks
- 1 cup heavy cream

Directions:

1. Stir the lemon juice, zest, and sugar until the sugar is dissolved. Whisk the egg yolks plus cream until blended in a large bowl. Stir in the lemon juice mixture. Scrape the mixture into four ½-cup

custard cups or ramekins. Put a rack in the insert of a large slow cooker. Put the cups on the rack.

2. Put within 1 inch of hot water into the cooker. Cook on high within 2 hours, or until the creams are softly set and slightly jiggly in the center. Uncover and let stand for 10 minutes. Carefully remove the cups from the cooker. Refrigerate within 2 hours, or up to 3 days, before serving.

Nutrition: Calories: 192 Carbs: 20g Fat: 11g Protein: 4g

266.   Bittersweet Chocolate Creams

Preparation time: 15 minutes
Cooking time: 1 hour & 30 minutes
Servings: 8

Ingredients:

- 2 tablespoons sugar
- 3 large eggs
- 2 cups heavy cream
- ¼ cup espresso or strong coffee
- 8 ounces bittersweet (not unsweetened) chocolate, broken into small pieces
- 1 teaspoon vanilla extract
- Chocolate-covered coffee beans (optional)
- Whipped cream (optional)

Directions:

1. Beat the sugar, eggs, cream, and espresso in a heatproof bowl that will fit in the slow cooker until blended and the sugar is dissolved. Add the chocolate and stir well. Place a rack in the insert of a large slow cooker. Place the bowl on the rack. Pour hot water around the bowl to a depth of 1 inch.
2. Cover and cook on high for 1½ hours, or until the chocolate is melted and the surface appears foamy. Carefully remove the bowl from the cooker. Whisk the mixture until blended. Add the vanilla. Spoon the mixture into eight ramekins or demitasse cups. Refrigerate until chilled and serve plain or garnished with the coffee beans and whipped cream.

Nutrition: Calories: 170 Carbs: 16g Fat: 13g Protein: 3g

267.   Bistro Crème Caramel

Preparation time: 15 minutes
Cooking time: hours
Servings: 8

Ingredients:

- 1 cup of sugar
- ¼ cup of water

- 1 12-ounce can evaporate whole milk
- 1 14-ounce can sweeten condensed milk
- 4 large eggs
- 1 teaspoon vanilla extract

Directions:

1. Mix the sugar plus water in a saucepan. Cook on medium heat, swirling the pan until the sugar is dissolved. Simmer, then gently swirl the pan until the syrup is evenly caramelized. Protect your hand with an oven mitt and put the hot syrup into a 6-cup soufflé dish.
2. Let it cool until the caramel is just set. Whisk the evaporated and condensed milk in a large bowl. Mix in the eggs plus vanilla until blended. Pour the mixture into the soufflé dish.
3. Put a rack inside a large slow cooker, then arrange the dish on the rack. Put hot water around the dish to a depth of 1 inch. Cover and cook on high within 2 to 2½ hours, then remove. Let it cool in the fridge within several hours or overnight. Cut into wedges and serve.

Nutrition: Calories: 136 Carbs: 24g Fat: 3g Protein: 4g

2-WEEK MEAL PLAN

Day	Breakfast	Lunch	Snack	Dinner	Dessert
1	Egg & Vegetable Breakfast Casserole	Butcher Style Cabbage Rolls- Pork & Beef Version	Piedmont Fontina Cheese Dip with Truffle Oil Fonduta	Greek Style Lamb Shanks	Apple Olive Cake
2	Breakfast Stuffed Peppers	One-Pot Oriental Lamb	Coarse Pork Terrine with Pistachios	Homemade Meatballs & Spaghetti Squash	Strawberry Basil Cobbler
3	Slow Cooker Frittata	Zucchini Lasagna with Minced Pork	Chicken Liver Pâté with Button Mushrooms	Beef & Cabbage Roast	Pumpkin Pecan Bread Pudding
4	Cranberry Apple Oatmeal	Stuffed Bell Peppers Dolma Style	Warm Tuscan White Bean Salad	Simple Chicken Chili	Chocolate Fondue
5	Blueberry Banana Steel Cut Oats	Slow BBQ Ribs	Stuffed Garlic Mushrooms with Cream and White Wine	Beef Shoulder in BBQ Sauce	Chocolate Orange Volcano Pudding
6	Berry Breakfast Quinoa	Steak & Salsa	Spanish Tortilla with Piquant Tomato Salsa	Moist & Spicy Pulled Chicken Breast	Nutella Fudge
7	Mediterranean Crockpot Breakfast	Beef Pot Roast with Turnips	Vine Leaves Stuffed with Rice, Herbs, Pine Nuts and Raisins	Whole Roasted Chicken	Greek Yogurt Chocolate Mousse
8	Slow Cooker Mediterranean Potatoes	Chili Beef Stew	Spanish Mackerel with Roasted Red Peppers	Pot Roast Beef Brisket	Peanut Butter Banana Greek Yogurt Bowl
9	Mediterranean Crockpot Quiche	Pork Shoulder Roast	Piedmont Fontina Cheese Dip with Truffle Oil Fonduta	Seriously Delicious Lamb Roast	Banana Foster
10	Slow Cooker Meatloaf	Easy & Delicious Chicken Stew	Coarse Pork Terrine with Pistachios	Dress Pork Leg Roast	Rice Pudding
11	Crockpot Chicken Noodle Soup	Chili Con Steak	Chicken Liver Pâté with Button Mushrooms	Rabbit & Mushroom Stew	Bittersweet Cocoa Almond Cake
12	Hash Brown & Cheddar Breakfast	One-Pot Chicken and Green Beans	Warm Tuscan White Bean Salad	Italian Spicy Sausage & Bell Peppers	Walnut Cake with Cinnamon Syrup
13	Slow Cooker Fava Beans	Two-Meat Chili	Stuffed Garlic Mushrooms with Cream and White Wine	Chicken in Salsa Verde	Sunny Orange Cake with Orange Syrup
14	Pork Sausage Breakfast	Slightly Addictive Pork Curry	Spanish Tortilla with Piquant Tomato Salsa	Salmon Poached in White Wine & Lemon	Two-Berry Clafouti

CONCLUSION

The Mediterranean is a prominent place. Dozens of different cultures and languages and cuisines blend together, but this and its lush climate are part of the reason it's such a culinary powerhouse today. It's a bounty for both the soul and the body, fit for a peasant or an emperor. Hopefully, this carried you to wherever you wanted to be – whether that was health, performance, or simple curiosity.

This cookbook was not intended to be the be-all-end-all publication on Mediterranean food, but it was structured to serve as a knowledge basis – to give you a complete idea of the most basics of where to look when it comes to making choices for yourself. Just the essentials and then enough to get you started, with enough to carry you in confidence. We also tried to give you a reliable, calorie-precise guide to what you'll be eating, not so you can obsessively track every calorie, but so you can start thinking about the food choices you make every day in hopes that it will encourage you to find your way to a healthy lifestyle.

Changing your diet isn't a simple thing, but hopefully, we'll provided enough examples to inspire you on a culinary journey. Cooking and eating is a fundamental part of existence, and it is also one of the most rewarding for the body and spirit.

We emphasize how the Mediterranean diet and slow cookers can be a beautiful combination if you want to try a healthier version of the food you eat. Slow cooking can be a radical change to those that have lived their entire lives hectically and impatiently. However, once you get used to the genuine taste that great food can deliver through a slow cooker, you will quickly adjust your schedule.

Quicker and faster is not always better, especially when it comes to instant food or fast foods, which is unhealthy, as we have seen in an overweight society and harnesses several ailments. This was designed to learn the basics and assets that slow cooking can bring to your life with a little twist of Mediterranean cuisine. You will find that there is no extra burden of time placed upon your schedule but a simple rearrangement of habit.

Once you have this new form of cooking blended into your routine, several cookbooks are designed for specific weight-loss diets, diabetic slow cooking, or even going Vegetarian. A slow cooker is one of the best and fabulous appliances that you can own. Follow the 2-week plan for putting menus in place and discover that you have more time than you did by opening a box and preparing the contents. You will find yourself switching to healthier foods, saving on groceries, and using less energy.

The slow cooker can be an essential part of your life when you realize the multiple advantages it provides in cooking healthy meals. Keep this cookbook handy and learn why slow cooker cooking is making such a famous comeback. You will discover that the slow cooker has always been a valuable tool, but perhaps, a little ahead of its time, for being noticed and appreciated.

At the very least, we have enriched your life in the smallest way. Enjoy your Mediterranean meals with your friends and family to the best effect. Whatever you've gleaned from this cookbook, the one thing we must say is Bon appétit!

9 781953 693921